# MAKING
# SENSE
# OF
# MARILYN

# MAKING SENSE OF MARILYN

## ANDREW NORMAN

FONTHILL

Fonthill Media Language Policy

Fonthill Media publishes in the international English language market. One language edition is published worldwide. As there are minor differences in spelling and presentation, especially with regard to American English and British English, a policy is necessary to define which form of English to use. The Fonthill Policy is to use the form of English native to the author. Andrew Norman was born and educated in the UK; therefore British English has been adopted in this publication.

Fonthill Media Limited
Fonthill Media LLC
www.fonthillmedia.com
office@fonthillmedia.com

First published in the United Kingdom and the United States of America 2018

British Library Cataloguing in Publication Data:
A catalogue record for this book is available from the British Library

Typeset in 10.5pt on 13pt MinionPro
Printed and bound by CPI Group (UK) Ltd, Croydon, CR0 4YY

*By the Same Author*

*By Swords Divided: Corfe Castle in the Civil War* (Halsgrove, 2003)
*Dunshay: Reflections on a Dorset Manor House* (Halsgrove, 2004)
*Sir Francis Drake: Behind the Pirate's Mask* (Halsgrove, 2004)
*Thomas Hardy: Christmas Carollings* (Halsgrove, 2005)
*Enid Blyton and her Enchantment with Dorset* (Halsgrove, 2005)
*Agatha Christie: The Finished Portrait* (Tempus, 2007)
*Tyneham: A Tribute* (Halsgrove, 2007)
*Mugabe: Teacher, Revolutionary, Tyrant* (The History Press, 2008)
*T. E. Lawrence: The Enigma Explained* (The History Press, 2008)
*The Story of George Loveless and the Tolpuddle Martyrs* (Halsgrove, 2008)
*Father of the Blind: A Portrait of Sir Arthur Pearson* (The History Press, 2009)
*Agatha Christie: The Finished Portrait* (Tempus, 2006)
*Agatha Christie: The Pitkin Guide* (Pitkin Publishing, 2009)
*Jane Austen: An Unrequited Love* (The History Press, 2009)
*Arthur Conan Doyle: The Man behind Sherlock Holmes* (The History Press, 2009)
*HMS Hood: Pride of the Royal Navy* (The History Press, 2009)
*Purbeck Personalities* (Halsgrove, 2009)
*Bournemouth's Founders and Famous Visitors* (The History Press, 2010)
*Jane Austen: An Unrequited Love* (The History Press, 2009)
*Thomas Hardy: Behind the Mask* (The History Press, 2011)
*Hitler: Dictator or Puppet* (Pen & Sword Books, 2011)
*A Brummie Boy goes to War* (Halsgrove, 2011)
*Winston Churchill: Portrait of an Unquiet Mind* (Pen & Sword Books, 2012)
*Charles Darwin: Destroyer of Myths* (Pen & Sword Books, 2013)
*Beatrix Potter: Her Inner World* (Pen & Sword Books, 2013)
*T.E. Lawrence: Tormented Hero* (Fonthill, 2014)
*Agatha Christie: The Disappearing Novelist* (Fonthill, 2014)
*Lawrence of Arabia's Clouds Hill* (Halsgrove, 2014)
*Kindly Light: The Story of Blind Veterans UK* (Fonthill, 2015)
*Jane Austen: Love is Like a Rose* (Fonthill, 2015)
*Thomas Hardy at Max Gate: The Latter Years* (Halsgrove, 2016)

# Preface

The world continues to be fascinated with Marilyn Monroe, who dazzled with her beauty and captivated the hearts of millions worldwide with her innocence, charm, generosity, and kindness, and yet, who died tragically at the age of only thirty-six.

However, Hollywood columnist, film critic, and author of *The Fifty Year Decline and Fall of Hollywood* Ezra Goodman, writing in 1961, the year prior to Marilyn's death, declared: 'The riddle that is Marilyn Monroe has not been solved'.[1]

> She impresses many people who know her quite well as being an enigma, and among the many people to whom I have talked in the course of gathering this material, not one really claimed to have the answer to that enigma. Putting together any sort of remotely searching story about Marilyn Monroe takes on all the aspects of a pathological detective story.

Finally, concluded Goodman, 'the difficulties in the way of ascertaining the facts about Monroe are many'.[2]

The life and death of Marilyn Monroe certainly raises some interesting questions. She gave the impression that she was an orphan and that her success was a rags-to-riches story. Yet this was not strictly true. Nevertheless, it cannot be denied that during her childhood she was sent to live with various other families, or in foster homes. This was because her father had disappeared from the scene and her mother had not the financial means to support her. How did this affect her later life, if at all? This will be discussed shortly.

Each of Marilyn's three marriages were attended by a degree of happiness, but this proved to be only temporary and none of them lasted for more than four years. However, this is perhaps not unusual among the film and theatrical community.

There has been much debate about the frame of mind that Marilyn was in when, on the night of 5 August 1962, she knowingly, or unknowingly, took her own life. Was it mental illness and instability, perhaps inherited from her mother Gladys, who in her thirties was diagnosed with schizophrenia, which led Marilyn to an increasing reliance on drugs (and drink), until finally she died from a self-administered excess of them? Or was she under the influence of forces beyond her control? Had her psyche, right from the beginning, contained the seeds of her own destruction?

## Authenticity of Material Relating to Marilyn

Can Marilyn's autobiography, *My Story*, by 'Marilyn Monroe with Ben Hecht (US playwright, journalist, screenwriter, director, and producer)', first published on 1 May 1974, be regarded as an authentic document? The history of the book is as follows.

On 16 March 1954, Marilyn wrote to Ben Hecht, confirming their agreement that he should 'write the story of [her] life to date, using material concerning [her] life which [she] had heretofore given [Hecht] for that purpose'.[3]

However, Hecht died on 18 April 1964, and when *My Story* was published a decade later, it ended with the line, 'This is where Marilyn's manuscript ended when she gave it to me', followed by the signature of fashion and celebrity photographer, 'Milton H. Greene' (i.e. not Ben Hecht).[4]

Marilyn's biographer, Donald Spoto, stated:

> It is clear that none of the first sixty-six pages of *My Story* was composed by Hecht at all. [And Spoto referred to] the final reworking of the text in the early 1970s by Milton Greene and an unknown writer or writers engaged by him.[5]

Aside from the fact that Marilyn's so-called autobiography cannot be relied upon, making sense of her is problematical, not least because in her early years she was insecure and introspective and unable even to make sense of herself. Her mother, Gladys, deliberately kept the identity of her father secret from her, and also from her half-sister and half-brother. Furthermore, she was misled as a child into believing that her foster parents were her real mother and father. Finally, in order to facilitate her pathway to fame, Marilyn, by her own admission, invented stories about herself, and others invented stories about her, for their own ends.

As Marilyn began to be successful, it was put about that she was a kind of modern-day Cinderella—a poverty-stricken orphan who had gone from rags to riches. This suited both the magazine proprietors who published photographs and wrote articles about her, and the film moguls in whose films she featured, for whom it was simply a publicity stunt designed to generate interest rather than be truthful. As for Marilyn and her family and close friends, they went along with a great deal of this narrative until the press finally discovered the truth.

Those who relied for their knowledge of Marilyn on the early films in which she featured, where in a succession of bit parts, she was portrayed as a glamorous but dumb blonde, would not have known that she was well read and wrote beautiful and insightful poetry.

However, trustworthy and reliable first-hand accounts of Marilyn do exist. For example, *The Secret Happiness of Marilyn Monroe*—her first husband James Dougherty's biography of her; Arthur Miller, her third husband's autobiography, *Timebends*; *The Fifty Year Decline and Fall of Hollywood* by Ezra Goodman; *Marilyn: Her Life in her Own Words*, by photographer George Barris of New York City; together with statements by her half-sister Berniece Miracle (*née* Baker).

Following Marilyn's death, Inez Melson, Marilyn's business manager (from 1954 to 1956), was appointed by attorney Aaron R. Frosch (who was a witness to Marilyn's will) and the court to act as administrator. Inez made a bonfire of Marilyn's papers, said Berniece Miracle, and 'Marilyn had tons of papers of all kinds'.[6] However, on the positive side, it is thanks to Inez that two filing cabinets containing Marilyn's personal effects were saved for posterity.[7]

Finally, film documentaries of the life and death of Marilyn contain invaluable, first-hand, eyewitness accounts from such important people in her life as George Barris, Hyman Engelberg, Eunice Murray, and Cyd Charisse.

In this way, by teasing out what is authentic from what is inauthentic, it is possible to shed new light on the enigmatic character of Marilyn Monroe, who is regarded, arguably, as the world's most famous ever movie star.

To make sense of this complex, endlessly fascinating, and all too fragile person, it is necessary to embark on a journey that proves to be both rewarding, and an infinitely moving experience.

# CONTENTS

# Birth, Parents, Forebears

## The Birth of Marilyn

Marilyn was born at Los Angeles General Hospital at 9.30 a.m. on 1 June 1926. She was christened Norma Jeane Mortenson (Norma subsequently changed her name to Marilyn Monroe, which is the name by which she will generally be referred to in this volume).

According to Marilyn's birth certificate, her mother Gladys's details were as follows:

> Gladys Monroe [she used her maiden name] aged 24; birthplace—'Mex' [Mexico]; abode—'5454 W [Wilshire] Blv'd [Boulevard], L.A. [Los Angeles]'; occupation— 'Motion Picture Lab' [Laboratory]; 'Number of children born to this mother—3'; 'Number of children of this mother now living—1'.

Marilyn's father was stated to be Edward Mortenson, aged twenty-nine; residence, 'unknown'; occupation, 'baker'.[1]

## Inaccuracies in Marilyn's Birth Certificate

On Marilyn's birth certificate, her father's name is given as 'Mortenson', whereas the name of the man whom Gladys had married twenty months previously, on 11 October 1924, was in fact 'Mortensen' (which was his correct name).[2] Was this simply a misspelling on the part of the registrar?

## Unanswered Questions

Why was Gladys's maiden name entered on Marilyn's birth certificate? The statement that Gladys now had three children (including Marilyn) was correct, but why did she state that only one (i.e. Marilyn) was still alive, when, in fact, her two children by her previous marriage to John 'Jasper' Newton Baker—namely Robert and Berniece—were very much alive? Why was 'Mortensen', incorrectly spelt 'Mortenson'? Was the misspelling of Mortensen's name simply that? Finally, Mortensen's whereabouts were stated to be 'unknown'. Where was he?

In the absence of Mortensen, the registrar would have had to rely on Gladys for the above information. So had she tried to create something of a smokescreen, in respect of the true circumstances of Marilyn's birth and the true identity of Marilyn's father? The answer is probably yes, as will shortly be seen.

## Marilyn's Mother Gladys, and Gladys's Parents

Gladys's mother, Della Mae Hogan, was born on a farm in Brunswick County, Missouri, on 1 July 1876, to parents Tilford Marion Hogan and Jennie, *née* Nance. In the 1890s, Della's family moved west to California, and in 1899, she married Otis Elmer Monroe, a house painter, originally from Indiana.

In 1901, Della and Otis relocated to Mexico where Otis was employed by the Mexican National Railway. On 27 May 1902 at Porfirio Diaz, on the border of north-eastern Mexico, their daughter, Gladys Pearl Monroe, was born. Gladys subsequently stated that her father, Otis Elmer Monroe, had worked in Mexico 'with a paint crew for a railroad outfit. He was in charge of a crew of quite a few men'. She said that he was also an artist, and one of his paintings, a landscape, hung on her wall.[3]

In 1903, the family relocated from Mexico to Los Angeles (LA), where Otis found work with the Pacific Electric Railway. On 6 October 1905, Della and Otis's son, Marion Otis Elmer Monroe, was born. Five years later, in 1909, Otis died of 'paint poisoning'.[4]

On 7 March 1912, Della, now aged thirty-five, married Lyle Arthur Graves, who, like the late Otis, worked for the Pacific Electric Railway (as a switchman supervisor). On 17 January 1914, Della and Graves divorced, whereupon Della relocated to Venice, 16 miles west of LA on the shores of Santa Monica Bay.

## Gladys's First Marriage

Gladys' first husband was John 'Jasper' Newton Baker, a businessman from Kentucky, whom she married on 17 May 1917. Gladys described Baker as 'a lady's man' who 'drank too much'.[5] There were two offspring from the marriage: Robert

Kermit ('Jack', or 'Jackie') Baker, born 16 January 1918, and Berniece Inez Gladys Baker, born 30 July 1919.[6]

In 1921, Jasper and Gladys paid a visit to Baker's mother in Flat Lick, Knox County, Kentucky. However, on the journey, young Jack fell out of a car and seriously injured his hip.

On 20 June 1921, Gladys filed for divorce. The divorce was finalised on 11 May 1923 and Gladys was given custody of her children. Berniece later described how, despite the court's ruling, Baker promptly abducted Robert and herself and took them to Kentucky.[7] Following this, Gladys hitchhiked to Kentucky and arrived at Flat Lick, where Baker was currently living with his mother. She was 'furious and intent on reclaiming her children'.[8] However, Robert was currently a patient in hospital in Louisville, having his injured hip attended to. Gladys, therefore, settled in Louisville, found employment as a housekeeper, and waited for Jack's condition to improve. Meanwhile, Baker was remarried to Maggie Hunter, *née* Mills.

When Gladys asked Baker's sister, Myrtle, to help her 'in stealing' Robert and Berniece, Myrtle 'refuses to help. Instead she races to alert Jasper'[9] who hitherto had thwarted all Gladys's efforts to see her children. Finally, Gladys gave up and returned to LA where she found employment as a film cutter at Consolidated Film Industries, Hollywood, LA.

The account of how Gladys was deprived of her young children and the noble, but futile attempts that she made to re-establish contact with them, is a truly heart-breaking one.

By summer's end 1923, Gladys was sharing an apartment (1211 Hyperion Avenue, East Hollywood) with Grace McKee, a colleague of hers who was a supervisor at Consolidated Film Industries.

## Gladys's Second Marriage

Their certificate of marriage states that Martin E. 'Edward' Mortensen (spelt correctly) and Gladys Pearl Baker were married on 11 October 1924 at Hollywood, LA; Mortensen was aged twenty-seven and Gladys aged twenty-two (which was correct), and for both of them, this was to be their second marriage. Also, both were residents of LA: Mortensen's address being '721½ W [West] Santa Barbara', and Gladys's '1211 Hyperion Avenue'. Mortensen was stated to be a native of California and Gladys, a native of Mexico. Gladys is described as 'Negative cutter at Studios', and Mortensen as a 'Meterman' (for the Southern California Gas Company). Finally, Mortensen's father and namesake Martin Sr's birthplace was stated to be Norway.[10]

Again, the marriage did not last, and seven months later, on 26 May 1925, Gladys left her husband and went to live again with Grace McKee. Mortensen, as plaintiff, immediately filed for divorce. It was alleged that Gladys, 'disregarding the solemnity of her marriage vows, willfully and without cause deserted plaintiff and ever since has and now continues to willfully and without cause desert and abandon plaintiff against his will'.[11]

When, in late 1925, Gladys learned that she was pregnant, she left Grace and took up residence at 5454 Wilshire Boulevard, LA.

## The Identity of Marilyn's Father

Given that Marilyn was born on 1 June 1926, and assuming that she was born at full term, then her date of conception would have been 9 September 1925, or thereabouts, i.e. more than eight months after her mother Gladys's separation from Mortensen.

A quarter of a century later, in 1952, a conversation took place between Berniece (who was now married to Paris Miracle) and Gladys. Berniece asked Gladys for details of Marilyn's father, to which the reply came, 'Marilyn's father was an important man in the movie industry'.

'Wasn't her father Edward Mortensen?' asked Berniece.

'No'.

'Does Marilyn know that?', Berniece continued.

'Yes, I told her. Grace told me to tell her.'

'When did you tell her?'

'Oh, I don't know, not too long ago.' When Berniece asked why she had not informed Marilyn of this before, Gladys replied, 'I told Marilyn that Grace said we should wait until she was old enough to understand.' Meanwhile, 'if Marilyn wants you to know', said Gladys, 'she can tell you.'[12]

Charles Stanley Gifford was foreman of the day shift at Consolidated Film—the company for whom Gladys worked as chief negative cutter. He had separated from his wife, Lilian, *née* Priester, in October 1923 and their divorce was finalised in May 1925.[13] By late 1925, Gifford and Gladys had become lovers, and it transpired (as will shortly be seen) that it was he who was Marilyn's real father.

As for Marilyn, 'My mother once told me my father died in an accident when I was quite young', she told photographer George Barris.[14] Marilyn's biographer, Michelle Morgan, explained how this may have come about. Gladys, she said, had been told in 1929 that Marilyn's father had been killed in a car crash: However, 'it later transpired that it was a completely different person who had died, and her ex-husband was actually alive and well and living in California'.[15]

Biographer of show-business personalities Maurice Zolotov referred to 'a report from the Salvation Army to the Mortenson family', which stated:

Our officer in Youngstown, Ohio, has called on the City Record Office and learnt that Edward Mortenson [note spelling] was killed on June 18, 1929, at 5.10 p.m. He was driving along the road leading from Youngstown to Akron. When he tried to pass a car in front of him, he crashed into a Hudson sedan. He was buried in Mt. Hope Park, Youngstown. The deceased did not leave anything of value.[16]

In fact, said Zolotov, writing in 1961:

Recently, two persons—one a friend of Marilyn's and the other an associate of hers—assured me that her father [i.e. Charles Stanley Gifford] is living, that his real name is not Mortenson, and that he is a well-known citizen of Los Angeles.[17]

Did Gladys genuinely believe—albeit erroneously—that the 'Mortenson', who had died in a road traffic accident in 1929, was Mortensen, whom she had married as her second husband? If so, what she told Marilyn was said in good faith. If not, did she deliberately mislead Marilyn by concealing from her the identity of her real father with whom she, Gladys, wished her daughter to have no contact whatsoever? If this was the case, it would have suited Gladys, at any rate for the time being, to pretend to Marilyn that Mortensen was her father and that he was now deceased.

# 2

# Childhood

On 13 July 1926, twelve days after Marilyn's birth, she and her mother Gladys, were discharged from hospital and they returned to Gladys's apartment—5454 Wilshire Boulevard.[1] Said Marilyn:

> … when Mother brought me home from the hospital—Grace and Mother hadn't been living together for a while, and Grace didn't even know I had been born; in fact, nobody did—well, anyway, Mother didn't have a crib to put me in, so she pulled out the dresser drawer in her bedroom and made me a little bed in the drawer.[2]

However, only a few days later, mother and baby relocated to 459 East Rhode Island Avenue, Hawthorne (situated 15 miles south-west of LA): a 'comfortable, small bungalow with electric lights and city water and an indoor toilet'.[3] Incidentally, this was the same street in which Gladys's mother, Della, lived.

This was the home of Albert Wayne Bolender and his wife, Ida, who were evangelical Christians. The Bolenders already had a foster child, Lester Flugel, who was of a similar age to Marilyn. They would now become Marilyn's foster parents. In return, Gladys would pay the Bolenders $25 a month for the keep of herself and her baby.[4]

According to Berniece, it was because Gladys was 'completely without means' that she was obliged to 'find someone to care for her infant daughter so that she can return to work'.[5]

Marilyn subsequently explained why her mother Gladys had not asked Della to look after her instead of the Bolenders. She said:

> I guess my grandmother was just too sick with malaria to keep me. When she went to Borneo with her husband … she got malaria. They told me she was often delirious with fever.[6]

Della had gone to Borneo on 20 March 1926 to join her gentleman friend Charles W. Grainger, who worked for an oil company. On 8 September 1926, three months after Marilyn's birth, Della returned from Borneo.

On 6 December 1926, Marilyn was baptised.

On 23 August 1927, Della died in Norwalk State Hospital for the Mentally Ill, LA (founded by the State Lunacy Commission in 1916).

In late 1927, Gladys, who had found it impracticable to commute to work from Hawthorne, returned to Hollywood to live with her friend and work colleague Grace McKee at Rayfield Apartments, 237 Bimini Place, LA; she left Marilyn in the care of the Bolenders.[7] However, Gladys visited her daughter frequently, taking her on walks and picnics and also to live, outdoor shows.

Grace McKee was born Clara Grace Emma Atchinson on 1 January 1894 in Montana. In 1915, she married Reginald A. Evans, an employee of the Shell Oil Company; he died four years later. In 1920, she married John W. McKee, a draftsman. Shortly afterwards, the couple separated and their divorce was granted in 1923.

On 15 August 1928, Gladys's divorce from Mortensen was finalised.[8] In September 1929, Marilyn commenced at Hawthorne Community Sunday School. In September 1931, Marilyn commenced at the Ballona Elementary and Kindergarten School, Hawthorne.[9] Berniece stated: 'Her closest companion is Lester, a foster child of the Bolenders, whom they eventually adopt'.[10] Lester was three months or so younger than Marilyn, and the two were brought up as brother and sister.

> Norma Jeane is healthy, strong, athletic, and keeps pace with Lester in their backyard contests. As she builds memories, she banks the fond affection of the Bolenders, the delight she feels wearing the fancy dresses that Ida sews for her, and a sense of accomplishment as she takes piano lessons.[11]

In September 1932, Marilyn commenced at Vine Street Elementary School, Hollywood (6 miles north-west of LA).[12] In September 1933, she commenced at Selma Avenue School, LA.

Photographs exist of Marilyn as a child, smiling radiantly and performing handstands on the beach at Santa Monica in the company of the Bolender family, and rowing a boat across a lake.

In June 1933, Gladys removed Marilyn from the Bolender household and brought her to Hollywood to live with an English couple who were minor actors and 'movie stand-ins'. They were George and Maude Atkinson, and they had a twenty-year-old daughter, Nellie.[13] The Atkinsons were from Yorkshire and had emigrated to the US in 1915. They lived at Afton Place, Hollywood, where they met Gladys in that same year.[14]

Marilyn described the Atkinsons to her biographer, US journalist George Carpozi. 'They were happy, jolly, and carefree.... They seemed like very nice people to me'.[15]

Meanwhile, Gladys took Marilyn to the theatre, and on an outing to Catalina Island (Santa Catalina, an island south of Long Beach and 22 miles from the coast of California). Marilyn would become reacquainted with Catalina shortly, as will be seen.

By the summer of 1933, Gladys, 'after scrimping for seven years' and working 'endless overtime hours', had finally saved enough money to make a down payment on a home for herself and her daughter. It was 'a two-storey house near the Hollywood Bowl [a venue for the arts, situated 8 miles north-west of LA]'.

Gladys subsequently told Berniece that 'she wanted to have a place so she could have all her children together. Norma Jeane and you and Jackie [Robert].[17] Alas, this would never be'.

On 16 August 1933, Marilyn's half-brother, Robert Baker, died of renal tuberculosis. When Grace McKee learned of the fact and visited Gladys to tell her the sad news, the latter 'refused to believe it'.[18] In September 1933, Gladys and Marilyn moved into their new abode: Number 6812 Arbol Street. This three-bedroomed house would be their first home of their own.

When Gladys purchased the property and took Marilyn in to live with her, said Grace, she was 'making good money'.[19] Furthermore, she presented her daughter with a piano 'to call her very own'.[20] However, in order to defray expenses, Gladys rented out a portion of her home to the Atkinsons, who continued to look after Marilyn when her mother was at work.[21]

In January 1934, Gladys's behaviour became somewhat erratic. She was admitted to a Santa Monica Asylum for several months and from there transferred to LA General Hospital. According to Grace, Gladys's illness began after she had purchased the house; she had 'trouble with the English couple' [the Atkinsons], and was then laid off from work. Within a few months 'Gladys had her nervous breakdown'.[22]

> The first I saw of it, one day she was lying on the couch.... There were steps in the living room leading upstairs—she started kicking and yelling, staring up at the staircase. She would lie there on her back and yell, 'Somebody's coming down those steps to kill me!' She was having delusions.

It was Grace's opinion that 'the house and all the responsibilities were just too much for her'.[23]

In September 1934, Marilyn, now aged eight, attended Selma Street School, Hollywood. In December 1934, Gladys was transferred to Norwalk State Hospital (where her mother Della had died eight years previously). On 15 January 1935, Gladys was declared insane. The diagnosis was paranoid schizophrenia, and the doctor noted: 'Her condition is characterized by religious preoccupations and a deep depression and some excitation; this condition seems to be chronic'.[24]

On 25 March 1935, Grace was appointed Gladys's legal guardian.[25] Meanwhile, Marilyn and the Atkinsons continued to reside at Arbol Street. On 27 May 1935, Gladys's house was placed on the market and Marilyn placed in the care of Elsie and Harvey Giffen of 2062 Highland Avenue, Hollywood. Harvey had been a colleague of Gladys's since the time when they had worked together at the film studio laboratory.[26]

On 12 June 1935, Gladys's house and furniture were sold, whereupon Grace's paternal aunt, Edith Ana Atchinson Lower—known as 'Aunt Ana'—purchased Marilyn's piano 'to hold in safe keeping for her'.[27]

On 10 August 1935, Grace married Erwin C. 'Doc' Goddard, an engineer and amateur inventor, and the couple invited Marilyn, now aged nine, to live with them at their new abode: a bungalow at 6707 Odessa Avenue, Van Nuys, north-west LA, Goddard was a divorcee who had custody of his three young children: Eleanor ('Bebe', born 1926); John ('Fritz', born 1928); and Nona Josephine (born 1930).[28]

However, the couple found that they could not afford to support the family and Marilyn. Therefore, on 13 September 1935, Grace arranged for Marilyn to be admitted to 'Hollygrove' Los Angeles County Children's Home—a residential orphanage located in Hollywood. In so doing, Grace was honouring Gladys's wish that Marilyn would neither be adopted nor taken out of the State of California.[29]

In respect of Marilyn, Grace stated: '[I] tried to keep her, but my schedule.... I couldn't keep her. I had to put her in the orphanage'.[30]

In September 1935, Marilyn returned to Vine Street School, and at weekends attended Sunday School at Vine Street Methodist Church.[31] By now, it had become clear that Gladys was 'not going to recover in the near future'.[32] On 27 March 1936, Grace became Marilyn's legal guardian.

On 7 June 1937, Marilyn was removed from the orphanage and returned to live with the Goddards at Van Nuys, whereupon Grace took her on a visit to the Columbia Studios of Columbia Pictures Corporation, Hollywood, where she herself was currently employed in the film library.[33]

Marital problems arose between Grace and her husband, Doc, so in autumn 1937, Grace decided that she and Marilyn would relocate to 237 Birmini Place, LA, the home of her sister, Enid Knebelkamp, and Enid's husband, Sam. Not long afterwards, Grace and Doc were reunited.

In December 1937, Grace placed Marilyn with Olive Monroe (*née* Brunings), the (presumed) widow of Gladys's brother, Marion Monroe. Marion had married Olive in 1924 and she had borne him three children: John 'Jack' Otis Elmer Monroe (born 1925); Ida Mae Monroe (born 1927); and Olive Elisabeth

Monroe (born 1929). On 20 November 1929, Marion left home. He was not seen again, and in 1939, he was officially declared deceased.

Olive resided in North Hollywood at the home of her mother, Ida (*née* Martin). Ida was a Christian Science practitioner: the Christian Science Church being a Christian sect that maintains that only God and the mind have ultimate reality. Marilyn now commenced at Lankershim School, North Hollywood.

On 3 March 1938, LA suffered a great flood and it became necessary to uproot Marilyn, yet again. This time she was placed with Grace's brother, Bryan Atchinson, and his wife, Lottie, and their daughter, Geraldine, of 1826 East Palmer Avenue, Glendale (8 miles north of LA).[34]

In autumn 1938, Gladys absconded from Norwalk State Hospital. She was now transferred to Agnews State Hospital, San José, near San Francisco. Situated 340 miles north-west of LA, the hospital had been founded in 1885 and was originally known as 'The Great Asylum for the Insane'.

In September 1938, Marilyn was uprooted yet again, and this time placed in the care of Grace's aunt, Edith Ana Lower, a fifty-eight-year-old divorcee of 11348 Nebraska Avenue, West LA.[35] According to Berniece, Marilyn 'idolize[d] Aunt Ana', attended the Christian Science church with her, and became an adherent of the faith in which Ana was a professional lay counsellor or practitioner.[36] Marilyn, now aged twelve, commenced at Sawtelle Boulevard School, West LA. She would now experience some of her happiest childhood times. Said Berniece:

> Going to the movies on Saturdays becomes Norma Jeane's favourite pastime, and, as she entered adolescence, fantasy life fills her private moments. She experiments with make-up for hours, and she acts out roles she has seen in films. Yet she has more success at school with athletics than with acting. Norma Jeane wins a track medal but is not cast in a play, although she does perform in a talent show.[37]

On 7 October 1938, Berniece married Paris Miracle of Pineville, Kentucky, and bore him a daughter, Mona Rae Miracle (born 1939).

It was in the winter of 1938, said Berniece (who was now aged nineteen) that she received a letter from her mother, Gladys, informing her that she had a twelve-year-old half-sister named Norma Jeane. 'She gave me the address so I could write to her if I wanted to'. The letter was written from Agnews State Hospital.[38] When Berniece informed Grace of this, the latter decided that the time had come to inform Marilyn, in turn, of Berniece's existence.

In September 1939, Marilyn, now aged thirteen, commenced at Emerson Junior High School, West LA. In that year, Grace joined the Christian Science Church.

By February 1940, owing to ill health, Ana Lower found herself unable to look after Marilyn. Following this, Marilyn returned to the Goddards, who were now living at 14743 Archwood Street, Van Nuys. Here, Marilyn enjoyed the company of the Goddards' daughter, Bebe, who was of a similar age. The house backed on to the home of the Dougherty family, which for Marilyn would prove to be highly significant, as will be seen.[39]

In September 1941, Marilyn (and Bebe) commenced at Van Nuys High School. The arrangement was that, after school, the two girls would walk to the Dougherty's house and wait there until James 'Jim' Dougherty arrived to take them home.[40] Dougherty was shortly to play a pivotal role in Marilyn's life.

In early 1942, the Goddards announced that they planned to move to West Virginia. When Marilyn was left behind, said Dougherty, it seemed to her like 'another rejection, another foster home that hadn't worked out. When Grace had taken her out of the orphanage to her last foster home, she told Marilyn that she would never have that kind of life again. But Norma Jean felt Grace had gone back on her word'.[41] (Dougherty spelt Marilyn's first name 'Jean', without the 'e'.)

Marilyn now returned to the home of her 'adored' Ana Lower. Grace said, '[I] wanted to stay with my Aunt Ana and get ready to marry Jimmy [Dougherty]'.[42] Marilyn now commenced at University High School, West LA, for a period of four months.[43] In March 1942, she accepted a proposal of marriage from Dougherty. She confided to Grace: 'Jim's such a wonderful person. I want to marry him, but I don't know anything about sex. Can we get married without having sex?'[44]

Prior to her marriage, said Dougherty, Marilyn 'made it clear that she was going to drop out of High School'. This was despite the fact that 'her social studies teacher, a man … told her she would be ruining her life'.[45]

Although Marilyn, as a child, was shunted about from pillar to post, her childhood was not an altogether unhappy one. It is said that the camera never lies, and in this regard, there are numerous photographs of her that appear to show that, at any rate in the context of the 'snapshots', she was happy and well looked after. On the other hand, it could be argued that it was only those who cherished her that chose to photograph her. These photographs include Marilyn as a baby, being cuddled by her foster mother Ida Bolender at Hawthorne, California in the summer of 1926;[46] Marilyn as a toddler, attired in a 'white voile dress covered with bright cherries and apples, with matching hat. Her clothing was made by Ida Bolender on her Singer machine'—this photograph, which was taken by her grandmother, Della, appeared in the *Los Angeles Times* of 7 April 1962;[47] Marilyn aged fourteen months, taken by Ida Bolender in the summer of 1927 and showing Marilyn dressed in a long white smock and looking radiantly happy;[48] Marilyn as a baby on Santa Monica beach, California, 1928; her mother, Gladys, sitting on the sand with her daughter nestling between her legs;[49] Marilyn as a toddler, with toy car and pointing with what appears to be a lollipop stick;[50] Marilyn, aged about two years, 'sitting in a wicker chair in a long white frilly dress, smart button up boots, and holding a big ball. Handwriting on the back of the photo identifies it as having been taken at a Hollywood Portrait Studio, and Gladys probably had the photo taken';[51] Marilyn aged three in 1929, sitting on a swing and smiling happily;[52] Marilyn, aged four, with Lester Flugel (another of the Bolenders' foster children), smartly attired with hair well groomed, in the garden holding hands, Marilyn with a coy smile on her face;[53] Albert Wayne and Ida Bolender, *circa* 1932, with four of their foster children, including six-year-old Marilyn, who is holding her pet dog 'Tippy';[54] Marilyn aged fourteen, with frilly dark hair, a radiant smile, and attired in blouse and cardigan;[55] and Marilyn aged fifteen, a pupil at Emerson Junior High School, LA, June 1941.[56]

# George Barris:
# Marilyn's Confidante

George Barris first met Marilyn in September 1954 in New York City when she was filming *The Seven Year Itch*. It was his idea to produce a book about Marilyn, illustrated with a 'series of my photographs of her'.[1]

Barris realised that in Marilyn, he was dealing with a thoroughly decent, sincere, and genuine person. He stated:

> She didn't act like a movie star. Although she was then twenty-eight, she looked and acted like a teenager. [She was] always polite and friendly to everyone on the set. She was no phony or snob.[2]

Did Marilyn tell the truth, in the account she gave to Barris? Barris stated:

> I believe so, even though, being an accomplished actress, she may have dramatized some events and added a bit of color to them—still the facts were there. Her eyes would tell me she was truthful, while her voice revealed the drama, so that I could feel the pain or joy she had gone through.[3]

As for Marilyn, she put her trust in Barris: a trust that proved to be fully justified, as will be seen, for she recognised that he was a rare human being, not to be counted among what she termed the 'Hollywood Wolves', who were trying to exploit and make money out of her.[4] The outcome was that Marilyn was more candid in her interviews with Barris than with anybody else, with the possible exception of her half-sister, Berniece. To Barris, she revealed all: her joys, sorrows, anguish, and it is thanks to their friendship that a greater insight is gained into her character than could ever otherwise have been the case. This is particularly true when she related to him the pleasures and pains of her childhood, the trauma she experienced over the loss of her home, and of being deprived of her mother's company, which was of especial poignancy.

Marilyn said to Barris:

> Lies, lies, lies, nothing but lies. Everything they've been saying about me is lies. You are the first one I'm telling it to. I'll tell you all about my childhood, career, marriages, and divorces—but most important, what I want most out of life.[5]

Marilyn was, however, stoical about those who misrepresented her. As regards 'those people that have been writing all those lies about me. I'm used to it, and [remember] the old saying: "consider the source".[6]

However, it was not until eight years later (in 1962) that Marilyn and Barris 'got around to seriously thinking about putting [their] book together'.[7]

## Identity of Marilyn's Father

Marilyn told Barris that her 'grandfather', by whom she meant Martin Mortensen Sr, father of her mother Gladys's second husband, Martin Jr, had been born in Haugesund, Norway: '[Martin Mortensen] and my grandmother met in Los Angeles after the First World War. My mother once told me my father died in an accident when I was quite young'.[8] This has already been referred to. In respect of her biological father, Marilyn said:

> [He] wasn't married to my mother when I was born. In fact he left my mother when he heard from her that I was on the way. His name: [Charles] Stanley Gifford. I was their love child. [In fact, Gifford and Gladys never married.] He told my mother that she should be glad she was married to Ed Mortenson [i.e. Mortensen]—at least she could give the baby his name. Stanley Gifford offered my mother money but she refused. She was willing to get a divorce and marry him, but he wouldn't do the right thing by her—even if she divorced her husband.[9]

Marilyn described Gifford as a 'divorced salesman' who had worked in the same film laboratory as her mother.[10]

This account was confirmed by Natasha Lytess of Columbia Pictures (she would one day become Marilyn's drama coach), who declared:

> Marilyn once told me that Grace McKee Goddard had told her that her father [i.e. Gifford] wanted to adopt Marilyn when she was a year or two old but that Marilyn's mother didn't let him because she hated him so.[11]

## Marilyn's Fond Memories of her Mother

Marilyn described to Barris the happy relationship that had existed between herself and Gladys, and said what an attentive and dutiful mother she was:

> When I was a small child, my fondest memories were being around my mother and her friends. It made me feel like we were one big happy family.
>
> Whenever Mom or her friends bought me an ice cream cone, we'd go for a walk or to the movies. I was in heaven when we went to church; I looked forward to this, even if it wasn't every week. There I was, dressed in my best clothes. Then, about noon, it was back home, where we always had a chicken lunch with our family— Mom and her friends. Then off we would go for a stroll, looking in the fancy store windows at things we couldn't afford to buy: we were dreamers.
>
> What made me sad was seeing other kids with their moms and dads strolling around holding hands. Oh, how I wished I had a dad, too. I know Mom loved me and tried to make my days happy ones, but most days she seemed sad and lonely.[12]

Gladys worked long hours, said Marilyn:

> [She] had to pay others to look after me. Sometimes I would get to see her only early in the morning or at night. It was enough for any mom to have a nervous breakdown. All I can remember was her being in and out of hospitals. But I never blamed her for my having to live in other homes. If only there was a daddy there to love and care for me.[13]

## Marilyn's Anguish when her Mother became Mentally Ill

Marilyn stated that she was only five years old, when her mother was 'sent to the hospital for a rest' and subsequently suffered a 'nervous breakdown': 'That's what caused me to spend my childhood in and out of foster homes.'[14]

## What Joy! Marilyn and her Mother are Reunited

Another cherished memory for Marilyn was when her mother, having been released from hospital, purchased a four-bedroomed house the following year into which both she and the English couple, the Atkinsons, were invited to live:

Then all seemed wonderful. She [Gladys] even bought me a piano at an auction that once belonged to the famous movie actor, Fredric March. I learned to play the classical tunes quite well. It's one of my best kept secrets—until now of course. Very few of my friends know I can play the piano. It came in handy when I played a duet on a piano with Tom Ewell, my co-star in *The Seven Year Itch*.

As a little girl, Marilyn stated:

I put on my Mom's clothes, tried to fix my hair as she did and powder my face with her big powder puff, and, oh yes, her red rouge and lipstick and eye shadow. I would imagine I was sexy, like the top movie star in those days, Jean Harlow.[15]

Grace was captivated by Jean Harlow, so Harlow was my idol too. I used to play act all the time. It meant that I could live in a more interesting world than the one around me. I read signed stories in fan magazines and believed every word the stars said in them. Then I tried to model my life after the lives of the stars I read about.

I used to go down to Grauman's Chinese theatre, and I'd say, 'Oh! Oh! My foot's too big!' I guess that's out. I'd stay there the whole day, and part of the evening, in the first row, a little girl all alone, looking up at the giant screen. And I adored it.[16]

When her mother's friends laughed at her, she said: '… Mom came to my rescue. That was my mother as I remember her. Always there when a little girl needs her mother'.[17]

Marilyn described 'being poor in those early years', but she had two priceless advantages: a loving mother, and the capacity to travel, in her imagination, to new worlds.[18]

I remember seeing Judy Garland in *The Wizard of Oz*. I sat there in a trance until my worried mother came to take me home. I asked her if there was another world out there or if it was just my imagination. Could dreams really come true? I wondered, are the movies a make-believe land, just an illusion.[19]

## Another Setback

'Tragedy struck again', said Marilyn, when her mother 'had another breakdown' and was committed to the Norwalk State Hospital, 'where she was in and out for several years'. Whereupon, at the age of nine, 'it was back to another foster home for me.' She was subsequently sent to live with Grace McKee.

## Grace McKee

Marilyn described Grace, whom she called 'Aunt Grace':

> [She was] my mother's best girlfriend. They worked together at the same film lab. She had promised my mother to always take care of me.[20]

However, it was not to be:

> I was living in the home of my mother's best friend [i.e. Grace]. Then she remarries. [This was Grace's third marriage.] All of a sudden her house became too small, and someone had to go. Guess who that someone had to be?[21]

## The Orphanage

Marilyn described to Barris how she cried when Grace took her to the Los Angeles Orphans Home, saying:

> Please don't let me stay here. I'm not an orphan—my mother's not dead. Please don't make me stay here. I was only nine years old then, but something like this I'll never forget. My heart was broken.[22]

However, Marilyn 'learned some time later' that Grace was also deeply distressed:

> The day Aunt Grace took me to the orphanage she cried all morning. She did make a promise to me that as soon as she was able to she would take me out of that place. Aunt Grace came to visit me often, but when a little girl feels lonely and that nobody cares or wants her, it's just something that she can never forget as long as she lives.

As for Grace's promise, Marilyn said, 'I didn't really believe her':[23] 'As nice as they tried to be to me at the orphanage, it never made up for the hurt that had been done by Aunt Grace. I wanted more than anything in the world to be loved'.

When, subsequently, Marilyn 'began to realize that what she did to me then hurt her so much', she forgave 'Aunt Grace'.[24]

## Happy Times with Ana Lower

After leaving the orphanage, said Marilyn, she lived with a succession of foster parents. Finally, at the age of eleven, she was sent by Grace to Grace's aunt, Edith

Ana Atchison Lower (known as Ana), a sixty-two-year-old spinster who lived at Van Nuys, which was described by Barris as 'a very poor neighborhood on the outskirts of Los Angeles'. Marilyn referred to her as 'Aunt Ana', and said:

> [She] became the greatest influence in my life. She was one of the few persons that I really loved with such a deep love that I could only have with someone so good, so kind, and so full of love for me.[25]
>
> I would go shopping with her. We were always looking for bargains, looking to save what little money Aunt Ana had.

For example, the pair used to stand in a long queue where 'for a quarter you could buy enough of the stale bread to last a week'.[26] Ana, however, encouraged Marilyn by smiling at her and telling her that when she grew up, she would be 'a rich, beautiful, and talented lady, a famous model and actress. Only [Gladys] and Aunt Ana knew these were [Marilyn's] secret dreams'.[27]

## Other Foster Homes

Marilyn had mixed memories of her numerous foster homes. On the one hand, for example: 'being forced to live in a closet for days … beatings, threats, housework, and the time when my foster parents held my head under the kitchen faucet when I was naughty'.

On the other hand, there were 'good things'. A 'cherished memory' of her childhood, Marilyn declared, was when she was fostered by an English couple (the Atkinsons), who had been in vaudeville (entertainment featuring musical and comedy acts) and who taught her 'how to juggle oranges, dance the hula, and how to play gin rummy. They even worked on improving [her] diction'.[28]

## High School

At Junior High School, Marilyn showed great strength of character in fending off her admirers:

> The boys knew better than to get fresh with me. The most they could expect was a good-night kiss on the cheek, and … if I really liked a boy he could give me a hug around the waist friendly-like.[29]

# 4

# The Legacy of Marilyn's Childhood

Marilyn could recall very little about her mother during the period of her childhood. However, she stated: '[I] remember her taking me to school.... She dressed me in a cute sailor outfit ... a little white pleated skirt with a navy middy blouse'. Marilyn also recalled: 'I sat at a huge black piano, and I took lessons ... but I really can't play'.[1]

Referring, presumably, to that time, Marilyn described:

> ... the lack of any consistent love and caring. A mistrust and fear of the world was the result. There were no benefits except what it could teach me about the basic needs of the young, the sick, and the weak.[2]

Marilyn said to George Carpozi:

> For many years I didn't know that my mother was alive. I could only remember her vaguely as a pretty woman who used to come and take me for rides while I was living with foster parents.
>
> The family I used to live with would tell me with dour faces that my mother was very sick and that I would not be able to see her for a long, long time. So I thought a lot about it and figured it out in my own mind that my mother was really dead.[3]

To what extent had those disruptive elements in Marilyn's childhood, as articulated by her above, influenced her subsequent development?

John Bowlby, British psychologist, psychiatrist, and psychoanalyst (1907–1990), described how Austrian neurologist Sigmund Freud, had 'insisted on the obvious fact that the roots of our emotional life lie in infancy and early childhood, but also sought to explore, in a systematic way, the connection between events of early years and the structure and function of later personality'.[4]

Bowlby himself agreed: 'The quality of the parental care which a child receives in his earliest years, is of vital importance for his [or her] future mental health'.[5] Bowlby made a distinction between physical neglect and emotional neglect. As regards the latter, he said, it was essential that 'an infant and young child should experience a warm, intimate, and continuous relationship with his mother, in which both find satisfaction and enjoyment'.

Child psychiatrists and many others now believed that 'it is this complex, rich, and rewarding relationship with the mother in early years, varied in countless ways by relations with the father and with the brothers and sisters [that] underlies the development of character and of mental health'.[6] It was the mother, said Bowlby, who 'feeds and cleans' the child, 'keeps him warm, and comforts him. It is to his mother that he turns when in distress'.[7]

Childhood suffering occurred, said Bowlby, because of 'the attitude of one of his parents, usually the mother', who was either 'overanxious or down on the child' (i.e. disapproved of him or was antagonistic towards him), or who was 'over possessive or rejecting' of him.[8] The term that Bowlby used to describe 'the state of affairs in which a child does not have this relationship' was 'Maternal Deprivation'.[9]

From 1969 onwards, Bowlby, together with US developmental psychologist Mary Ainsworth (1913–1999), developed and formulated their 'Attachment Theory'. This states that a strong emotional and physical attachment to at least one primary caregiver is critical to personal development. In most cases, of course, the primary caregiver to whom the infant becomes attached is the mother. Later, Bowlby said that from about the time of the child's first birthday 'other figures, for example father or grandmother, may become important to him, so that his attachment is not confined to a single figure'.[10] These 'other figures' may include the child's older siblings.

If one or both parents were 'persistently unresponsive to the child's care-eliciting behaviour' (i.e. cries for help), and were 'actively disparaging or rejecting', this could lead that child 'to live in constant anxiety, lest he lose his attachment figure'. This condition, said Bowlby, was best described as one of 'anxious attachment', in which there was likely to be 'much underlying resentment', accompanied by an 'unexpressed yearning for love and support'.[11]

Bowlby also described how a child's 'neurotic [i.e. stress-related] symptoms' may be 'made worse by separation from the mother'.[12] Finally, children who had 'apparently recovered from a separation experience' were 'particularly vulnerable to threats of separation' in the future.[13] This latter observation by Bowlby would be highly significant as far as Marilyn was concerned, as will shortly be seen.

In contrast with those who had suffered from maternal emotional deprivation, Bowlby continued, studies show that those individuals who have 'grown up in closely-knit families, with parents who ... have never failed to provide them with support and encouragement [become] self-reliant and successful, both in their human relationships and their work.[14] This, of course, is a generalisation, but in the main, it is undoubtedly true.

Bowlby stated that it was 'by no means clear' why some children who had experienced maternal emotional deprivation were damaged, and yet others were not, and it was possible that hereditary factors played a part.[15] Likewise, it was puzzling that separation induced high levels of anxiety in some children, but not in others.

Finally, Bowlby said:

> ... the requirement of an attachment figure, a secure personal base [was] by no means confined to children. There are good reasons for believing ... that the requirement applies also to adolescents, and to mature adults as well.[16]

To take Marilyn as an example: yes, she did have many happy times as a child, and love from both her mother and from at least a number of her foster parents— notably the ones who wished to adopt her.

Until her mother, Gladys, succumbed to mental disorder, Marilyn was cherished and cared for, both emotionally and materially, even though her household was by no means well off. Suddenly, everything changed. She was uprooted on numerous occasions, with all the uncertainty that this entailed, and therefore lacked the 'constant love' that she so craved. A particular trauma for her was being told that her mother was ill, but not being told the reason why, and finally, not even knowing if Gladys was still alive.

As for being able to bond, either with her biological father, Charles Stanley Gifford, or with Edward Mortensen (to whom her mother was married up until the time when Marilyn was aged two), this had proved to be impossible as neither man had featured, to any meaningful extent, in her life.

Neither was Marilyn able to bond with her half-brother, Robert, or with her half-sister, Berniece, for the simple reason that it was not until she was aged twelve that she learned of Berniece's existence; the pair did not meet for another six years, by which time Robert had already died.

Given such a background, it therefore seems likely, according to Bowlby, that Marilyn would become resentful, neurotic ('neurosis—a relatively mild mental illness ... involving depression, anxiety, obsessive behaviour, but not a radical loss of touch with reality'[17]), and desperately anxious to find an 'attachment figure' to whom she could relate, who would always be there for her, and upon whom she could utterly depend.

# Childhood Sexual Abuse, and Its Possible Consequences for Marilyn

Marilyn described how, when she was about eight years old and living in a foster home, the 'star boarder' was an old man who, on one occasion, called her into his room.

> I went in, and immediately he bolted the door. He asked me to sit on his lap. Frightened, I obeyed. He kissed me and started doing other things to me. He put his hand under my dress. He said it's only a game. He let me go when his game was over. He touched me in places no one had ever before.[1]

Marilyn explained what happened after she ran crying to her foster mother:

> ... she looked at me, shocked at what I had told her. She slapped me across the mouth and shook me, shouting, 'I don't believe you. Don't you dare say such nasty things about that nice man'.

From then on, Marilyn developed a stammer and a stutter.[2]

A possible long-term effect of childhood sexual abuse is post-traumatic stress disorder (PTSD), the features of which are as follows: anxiety, depression, poor concentration, irritability, flashbacks to the traumatic event in question, feelings of guilt, and recurrent and distressing dreams. However, because the abuse described by Marilyn above does not appear to have been sustained, and because, as will be seen, it did not progress to a full rape (defined as sexual intercourse with a person against their will), the likelihood is that its consequences were less severe than would otherwise have been the case.

# First Marriage:
# James Dougherty

The Dougherty family originated in Ireland and were 'driven out' by the Great Famine, 1845 to 1852.

James 'Jim' Edward Dougherty was born on 12 April 1921 in LA to Edward Dougherty, 'a toolmaker for mining equipment', and Ethel Mary, *née* Beatty. He was the youngest of four children. His parents were both from Colorado, but relocated to California, finally settling in Torrance in the south-west region of LA County.

In the late 1930s, the Dougherty family moved to 14747 Archwood Street, Van Nuys, where they found themselves near neighbours of Doc and Grace Goddard of 14743 Archwood Street. After moving here, Dougherty's mother, Ethel, and Grace became 'pretty close' friends.[1] James now became a pupil at Van Nuys High School, which was the same school that Marilyn attended—he was almost five years her senior.

After leaving school in 1939, Dougherty worked first as an embalmer for a funeral home and later as an employee of the Lockheed Corporation (headquarters Burbank, California).[2]

In September 1941, the Goddards, including Marilyn, moved 'a mile or so away to a more spacious and comfortable home': 6707 Odessa Avenue, Van Nuys. On 7 December 1941, the Japanese attacked Pearl Harbor, Hawaii. The following day, Japan declared war on both the US and the British Empire. On 11 December 1941, the Axis powers and the US declared war on each other.

Not long after these momentous events, Grace asked Dougherty if he would care to take Marilyn to a Christmas dance held by Doc Goddard's firm, Adel Precision Products of Burbank city, situated 12 miles north-west of LA.[3]

Referring to early spring 1942, Dougherty stated:

Mom called me aside one day and said Doc and Grace are going to have to move to West Virginia for his company. They're going to take Bebe [their daughter], but they can't take Norma Jean[e]. Mom came right to the point. 'Grace wanted to know if you would be interested in marrying her'. [Otherwise] Norma Jean[e] would have to return to the orphanage, since Aunt Ana felt she was too old to look after her—I said, 'Yes'.[4]

Dougherty said that it was early in 1942 that Marilyn left the Goddards and moved in with Aunt Ana Lower at her home, 11348 Nebraska Avenue, West LA. In March 1942, the Goddards duly relocated to 322 Wilson Court, Huntington, West Virginia.

Dougherty said that Ana and Norma Jeane became 'very close over the summer. Norma Jean had a great respect for people up in years [i.e. elderly]. They were always special to her. She had even entered Ana's church, which was of the Christian Science faith. It appealed to her feeling that nearly everyone was good'.[5]

Dougherty and Marilyn were married on 19 June 1942. The marriage took place at 432 South Bentley Avenue, West LA: '[This was] the home of the Goddards' friend Chester Howell, and this location was chosen 'because she [Marilyn] liked the winding staircase in their front hall, just like in the movies'.[6]

The service was conducted by the Reverend Benjamin Lingenfelder of the Christian Science church. It was Aunt Ana, who designed her wedding gown, Marilyn told George Barris. Talking of her wedding to Dougherty, Marilyn stated:

> I had six [former foster] mothers claiming me and all weeping when I marched down the aisle. I guess they all considered me their daughter even though they were my foster mothers only—at one time or another in my young life.[7]

On the couple's marriage certificate, Marilyn's details were stated as follows:

> [The Goddard] Name, 'Norma Jeane Mortensen'; Age, '16'; Address, '11348 Nebraska Avenue' [L.A.]; Occupation, 'none'; her father was 'E Mortensen', whose address was 'unknown'. Dougherty's details were stated as: Name, 'James Edward Dougherty'; Age, '21'; Address, '14747 Archwood [Street], L.A.'; Occupation, 'Shaper operator Lockheed AC [Aircraft Corporation]'.[8]

The newlyweds set up home in a furnished studio apartment, 4524 Vista del Monte, Sherman Oaks District, San Fernando Valley (16 miles north-west of LA). Said Dougherty of Marilyn: 'It was the first time in her life she'd had a real home of her own'. She also told him that 'she had had no childhood, and it showed', he said.[9]

Said Marilyn of Dougherty: 'my relationship with him was basically insecure from the first night I spent alone with him'.[10] Although Marilyn referred to herself as 'a girl 6 yr [years] younger', she was, in fact, just under five years younger than Dougherty. She told Barris:

> I didn't know anything about marriage, especially the sex part of it, and I was scared to death about what a husband would do to me.[11] [However] marriage to Jim brought me escape at the time. It was that or my being sent off again to another foster home. Once more it was the case of not being wanted. It wasn't fair to push me into marriage. What did I know about sex?[12]

In a typed account, composed by Marilyn, probably in late 1943, she described Dougherty as 'one of the few young men [she] had no sexual repulsion for'. She also said that she 'would never have stayed with him but for his love of classical music [and] his intellect which made a pretence at being more than it was'.[13]

Yet, to be fair, Dougherty was no slouch, as far as intellect was concerned, as this statement by him reveals:

> I was the Van Nuys team member in a Shakespearian Festival Contest at Occidental College and took first place in my class, reciting Shylock's 'revenge' speech [from William Shakespeare's play, *The Merchant of Venice*].[14]

Incidentally, Dougherty had also won a sports scholarship to an institute for higher education, which he had to forego in order to work to help support his parents. He later recalled the good times spent with Marilyn: 'Norma Jean[e] and I had a very normal, beautiful life while it lasted, which included friends, family, and the great outdoors—something she loved'.[15] Marilyn loved to fish and she would accompany him on hunting expeditions 'but would never shoot anything.[16] She could also row a boat. She told me she'd known how to row a boat since she was seven years old. Apparently, Mr Bolender, her first foster father, had taken her on occasional camping trips with Lester, their adopted son'.[17]

On 14 September 1942, Marilyn wrote to Grace to describe her wedding. She also indicated to Grace that she wished to establish a relationship with Charles Stanley Gifford, whom she believed to be her biological father. The letter begins: 'I want to thank you so much for writing Mom [Gladys] and explaining things about Stanley G. [Gifford]'. In a postscript, she wrote: 'How can I get in touch with Stanley Gifford? Through Consolidated Films, or something like that. Which dept?'[18]

In January 1943, when their lease ran out, the couple moved into the Dougherty family home at 14747, Archwood Street, Van Nuys. This they shared with James's brother, Tom. Meanwhile, Dougherty's parents, Edward and Enid, had relocated to Thousand Oaks, Ventura County, south-eastern California.[19] In spring 1943, Marilyn and Dougherty moved into a detached house: 14223 Bessemer Street, North Hollywood.[20]

Dougherty was anxious to play his part in the war effort, and in late 1943, he enlisted in the US Maritime Service, which trained people to become officers and crew members in merchant vessels of the US Merchant Marine. After basic training, Dougherty was posted to Avalon, Santa Catalina (which Marilyn had previously visited with her mother, as already mentioned), to the Merchant Marine Training School. When he invited Marilyn to join him there, she was overjoyed. 'I'll find us a place to stay here. You'll live here on Catalina,' Dougherty (who was equally delighted) told her.[21]

> On weekends, we'd go skin diving. She did love to swim and we spent a lot of time at the beach. I look back on that year on Catalina as the honeymoon we couldn't have when we first got married.[22]

Here at Catalina, Marilyn was taught weightlifting by Howard Corrington, a former Olympic weightlifting champion, 'as a way to improve her figure and her posture'.[23] As regards marital fidelity, she declared: 'I was always true to my husband, but he seemed jealous and annoyed when the men [of the training school] would whistle at me'.[24]

In spring 1944, when Dougherty was posted to the South Pacific, Marilyn moved in with his parents, who now lived at 5254 Hermitage Street, North Hollywood (15 miles north-west of LA).[25] As he prepared to embark, he said, '[Marilyn] sobbed quietly on my shoulder for a few minutes before I went up the gangplank.'[26] This was to be a year-long tour of duty, during which time Marilyn wrote to him 'nearly every day. They were mostly all love letters, about how much she missed walking with [him] up the hill to [their] apartment, about how lonely she was in bed at night'.[27]

In his absence, Dougherty said, Marilyn 'would confide in Mom and lean on her for support when I had been gone for months and she was lonely.'[28] Doc Goddard had helped Dougherty's mother, Ethel, get a job at Radioplane, Burbank, in the infirmary. This was an aviation company that produced drone aircraft for use as gunnery targets for training purposes. Marilyn asked Ethel if there was a chance that she might also be taken on there.[29]

> [The outcome was that] they started me there as a parachute inspector, and later I was promoted to 'the dope room', where I would spray this liquid dope, which is made by mixing banana oil and glue, on the planes' fuselages. These were miniature planes used for target practice.[30]

In fact, Marilyn worked with such dedication that she received an award from the company.

In late October 1944, Marilyn visited Grace, who was working in a film laboratory in Chicago, and Grace's daughter, Bebe Goddard, in West Virginia.

Afterwards, she met with her half-sister, Berniece Miracle, for the first time. Berniece and her family were now living in Detroit, Michigan. Following their meeting, Marilyn told Berniece in a letter, 'I love you dearly. I always shall, my own dear sister.'[31]

In late 1944, Dougherty returned home on leave. During this period, he said:

[Marilyn] suddenly announced that she was going to call her 'father' [Charles Stanley Gifford], a man she had never been in touch with before. Now, with Mom sitting on the living room sofa and me standing next to her, Norma Jean[e] picked up the phone and called the man whose identity she had discovered after tracking him down through people who had once worked with her mother at Consolidated Film Industries [where Gifford himself had once been an employee]. 'This is Norma Jean[e]', she said in a trembly sort of voice. 'I'm Gladys' daughter'. Then she slumped and hung up the receiver. 'Oh, honey!' she said. 'He hung up on me!'[32]

Marilyn described to Barris how, one day in December 1944, Army photographer David Conover arrived at the Radioplane plant:

He was from the army's pictorial center in Hollywood. His assignment was to take pictures for the army newspapers and magazines of people working in defense plants, showing them doing their share in the war effort. He called them morale-booster photos. Those pictures he took of me were the first that ever appeared in a publication. [They subsequently] appeared in hundreds of army camp newspapers, including the army's famous *Yank* magazine and *Stars and Stripes*.[33]

Conover showed the photographs that he had taken of Marilyn to Potter Hueth, 'a commercial photographer friend in Los Angeles'. The outcome was that an interview was arranged. 'Secretly I'd always wanted to be a photographer's model,' said Marilyn. The current fee was 'usually $5 to $10 an hour, which was a lot of money in those days'.[34]

In late January 1945, Dougherty embarked once more, for the South Pacific and the Far East.[35] On 15 March 1945, Radioplane cancelled Marilyn's contract. She now took on a further succession of modelling assignments.

Marilyn described how at about this time, she visited her mother, Gladys, at Agnews State Hospital in company with Ana Lower:

I almost wished I hadn't. I hadn't seen her in ten years [i.e. since January 1935, when Gladys was admitted to Norwalk State Hospital] and I was expecting ... I was looking forward ... she wasn't ... I didn't go again. She's not like my mother. Grace is like my mother. And Aunt Ana, even more than Grace.[36]

Gladys was 'really a stranger to me', said Marilyn:

Part of me wants to be with her ... and part of me is a little afraid of her. I went to see Mother because she seemed to have regained some interest in the outside world. You know, she'd told us about each other and she'd been wanting to get out of the institution. But the plain fact is she has never actually said to me, 'Come visit me,' just things like, 'get me out' [i.e. of hospital].[37]

Although Marilyn confessed to being angry with her mother, she said:

I know its irrational. I know with my head that she didn't mean to turn her back on me. She didn't purposely get sick. I try and try. The feeling makes my stomach hurt. Even when she was with me she wasn't there.[38]

In early June 1945, Marilyn wrote to Berniece to tell her that their mother, Gladys, 'will soon be released from the mental institution', and that she was 'thrilled at their mother's progress'.[39]

On 26 June 1945, David Conover photographed Marilyn for *Yank* magazine. That summer, the pair embarked on a visit to the Mojave Desert and Death Valley for a photo shoot. Had it not been for Marilyn becoming a model, following a meeting with a photographer from *Yank* (i.e. Conover), said Dougherty, 'I'm quite sure that Norma Jean[e] and I would still be married.'[40] In that summer of 1945, the Goddards returned to LA.

Dougherty wrote from Shanghai in late July 1945:

[He asked] if we could patch things up and make a go of our marriage.... I knew our marriage was over. A career was more important to me. I wanted to become an actress more than ever. Perhaps through modelling I would get the break I needed.[41]

Marilyn said:

My career as a model started when Potter Hueth showed the pictures he took of me to Miss [Emmeline] Snively, who then ran the largest model agency in Los Angeles. I was quite excited when she agreed to see me.[42]

This was the Blue Book Modelling Agency, which Miss Snively ran from the Ambassador Hotel, 3400 Wilshire Boulevard, LA. However, her husband, Dougherty, 'never wanted [her] to become a model or actress', said Marilyn: 'In fact he never encouraged me in any way'.[43]

On 2 August 1945, Marilyn was interviewed by Miss Snively and duly placed on her books as a model. She arranged for Marilyn to have lessons at her modelling school, which Marilyn could pay for 'out of the modelling jobs [Snively] would get for [Marilyn]'. Marilyn said:

I was then nineteen, my marriage was strained, and I was thinking of a divorce. When I wrote to my husband, I explained I did not love him anymore, that I had a chance for a career as a model, and that I wanted freedom to pursue my career. I wanted a divorce. Jim was still in Shanghai.[44]

Having attended two modelling assignments, she said:

I believed in myself so much that I would make it as a model, I quit my job at the defense plant [Radioplane].[45]

Then they started to put me in bathing suits, and all of a sudden I became popular. In those days I was a brunette, Miss Snively kept insisting I become a blonde.

Reluctantly, Marilyn agreed to be converted: '… to a golden blonde. I began to get more modelling assignments in photography for glamour poses, and especially cheesecake pictures'. (Cheesecake—images portraying women in a manner that emphasises idealised or stereotypical sexual attractiveness.[46])

In August 1945, Gladys was released from Agnews State Hospital, on condition that she reside with her Aunt Dora Graham at Portland, Oregon. According to Berniece, it was Dora who 'eventually got mother released'.[47] By this time, said Marilyn, 'I was already grown up. I remember how optimistic I felt in L.A. We were all so ecstatic that she was out, but she wouldn't let us get close to her. And I kept trying … we did things together … it was so impossible'.[48]

Dora subsequently spoke to Berniece about her mother:

[She] seems narrowly focused on a single tenet of the Christian Science philosophy and is intent on trying to cure sick people without the aid of medicine. Gladys has begun to dress in white as if she was a nurse: white uniform, white stockings, white shoes. She first takes short jobs near Dora, then accepts jobs farther and farther away.[49]

Said Ezra Goodman, 'the first "name" photographer to shoot Marilyn was André de Dienes', who was born in Transylvania 'and now lived in a modernistic house hanging over Hollywood's Sunset Strip. Monroe was sent to him by Snively and he was impressed'.[50]

Marilyn spent the December of 1945 in Death Valley, Yosemite, and Oregon, being photographed by de Dienes. She also spent Christmas 1945 with him, during a film 'shooting trip' to Washington State.[51] Said Barris, it was André de Dienes, 'one of the leading glamour lensmen of his day [whose] photos of Norma Jeane made the covers of the top magazines and brought national recognition to the then unknown young beauty'.[52] Such magazines included *Eye*, *Laff Magazine*, *Pageant*, *The Family Circle*, and *True Experiences*.

On 25 December 1945 (Christmas Day), de Dienes took Marilyn to visit her mother Gladys again; this time at Dora's home in Oregon.[53] Said she:

> When I went to see her … I felt so … lost. I drove up there thinking it was going to be one of the most joyful times in the world. Except for seeing her that once in the institution, I hadn't seen her since I was about nine years old. All those years I had waited and wished … but when I saw her, she wasn't loving or understanding. She was cold. I felt so let down. Unloved.[54]

Meanwhile, Dougherty remarked on growing tensions between his mother Ethel, and Marilyn:

> Mom didn't know how to begin to deal with Norma Jean[e]'s ambition. She may have even seen it as a kind of betrayal of her son, although she never said anything of that nature to me. So things became touchy around the house and finally, Norma Jean[e] [in September 1945] moved back to Aunt Ana's in West Los Angeles.[55]

According to Berniece Miracle, it was Miss Snively who recommended Marilyn 'to agent Helen Ainsworth of National Concert Artists Corporation, who assigns her to her associate Harry Lipton. Among Norma Jeane's credits by this time are covers for [magazines] *Laff, Peek, See,* and *U.S. Camera*'.[56] Marilyn signed a contract with Helen on 11 March 1946.

In April 1946, Marilyn sent Gladys some money in order that she might return to LA. When she did, mother and daughter moved into rented accommodation—i.e. two rooms situated beneath Ana Lower's apartment on Nebraska Avenue. Ana helped Gladys to find employment in a department store.[57]

In that same month of April 1946, Dougherty came home on leave and arrived at Nebraska Avenue, where Marilyn answered the door. She admitted him to the house, but when he peered round the bedroom door, there in the marital bed was Gladys.[58]

Dougherty recalled his first 'encounter' with Marilyn's mother, Gladys, who was dressed all in white, including nurse's white stockings and shoes.

> In fact, she looked more like a nurse than she did an ordinary civilian. I never did figure that out, since Gladys had gone overboard with Christian Science and didn't believe in doctoring. She was polite enough, but she didn't seem to connect with me at all. Her mind was out in left field [a U.S. expression meaning that the person was behaving oddly or strangely] somewhere. I never saw her angry and I never saw her laugh. She was very pious and apparently content.[59]
>
> [Marilyn, however,] greeted her mother more like a friend, a strange friend. [She] once told me that Gladys was 'like someone I don't know because I was so young when she left me.' She never had the feeling of 'This is my mother.'

Yet Marilyn did recall 'happy trips to the beach or just visits, from her early childhood'.[60] Dougherty said:

> [Marilyn had become] calculating, something she never had been before. She had made sure that Gladys would be living there on Nebraska Avenue when I made my last appearance, that her mother would have my place in the only bed in the apartment. I was part of the past she had turned her back on, although she was willing to give me some crumbs of her affection.[61]

To George Barris, however, Marilyn described how, at that time, her relationship with Gladys was warm and friendly on both sides. Said he:

> Her success as a model had enabled Norma Jeane to leave her Aunt Ana then and to move into her own small apartment [at Nebraska Avenue]. Her mother Gladys, had been released from a hospital stay and came to live with her daughter there. They slept in the same bed. Acting as her daughter's secretary, Gladys took phone messages and made appointments for her. For a while all was well.
>
> Gladys couldn't do enough for her daughter. She ran errands, went shopping, and even travelled by streetcar to the Ambassador Hotel, where Miss Snively's modelling agency was located, to thank her personally for being so helpful to Norma Jeane's career.[62]

Marilyn and Dougherty 'had a showdown':

> I thought I'd given her modelling career a fair trial, well over a year, and she was letting our home life slide more and more. So I just told her that she would have to choose between a modelling career and maybe the movies or a home life with me like we had in Catalina. Then she got very emotional. She said I was gone [i.e. away from home] too much. How could I expect her to be a housewife when I was at sea more than half the time? Catalina was wonderful, she said, but when are you coming home to stay?

Dougherty replied, 'Baby, I'll leave the Maritime Service just as soon as they'll release me'. The problem was, however, that '[he] had no prospects then of a decent job outside'.[63]

Dougherty's attempt at a reconciliation was to no avail. Marilyn informed him that 'she was going to be an actress. Her mind was made up'.[64] He spent the remainder of his leave with his parents at Thousand Oaks. How would Marilyn cope without him, Dougherty wondered, when her mother was 'a woman who was only capable of looking on passively and putting her trust in God?'[65]

On 14 May 1946, Marilyn visited Las Vegas, Nevada, where divorces could easily be obtained. Meanwhile, she appeared on the cover of various magazines, and in advertisements for shampoo, toothpaste, etc.

In late May 1946, when Dougherty was in Shanghai, China, he received a letter from Marilyn's Las Vegas attorney, informing him that Marilyn was filing for a divorce.[66]

Marilyn told Barris that US entrepreneur Howard Hughes, having seen her picture on the front of a magazine, had expressed an interest in her. When Ben Lyon, studio executive and 'talent agent' at Twentieth Century Fox Film Corporation, learned of this, he arranged for Marilyn to have a 'screen test in color'.[67] This was to be 'a silent test. There was no dialogue'.[68]

It was now that Marilyn's half-sister, Berniece, was reunited with her mother, when, on 14 August 1946, she and daughter, Mona Rae, arrived at LA for a three-month stay with Marilyn and Gladys.[69] When they arrived at Burbank Airport, not only Marilyn and Gladys, but also Ana Lower and Grace Goddard were there to meet them.

Berniece said:

When Norma Jeane has time off and on weekends, she takes Gladys, Berniece, and Mona Rae for drives during the course of which, they visited Beverly Hills (12 miles west of Los Angeles), Grauman's Chinese Theatre (Hollywood Boulevard, Hollywood, built in the Chinese style and opened in 1927), and the Hollywood Bowl.[70]

Berniece remarked that in her reading, Gladys was solely concerned with Christian Science: 'Since Ana [Lower] introduced her to it in the institution, she has become obsessed with discovering the possibilities of mind over illness'.[71]

Gladys criticised Marilyn for wishing to become an actress, saying, 'You ought to be something worthwhile'.[72] When challenged by Berniece, Gladys replied, 'I don't like her [Marilyn's] business'.[73] Marilyn, nevertheless, lived in the hope 'that [her] mother [would] act better when she has been on the outside longer'.[74] Meanwhile, Marilyn 'either models on assignments for Emmeline Snively's Blue Book Model Agency [located at the Ambassador Hotel, Los Angeles] or attends her classes at Fox'.[75] Here, girls were groomed for careers in films and photographic and fashion modelling.

On 26 August 1946, with the approval of studio head Darryl Zanuck, Marilyn, now aged twenty, was offered a contract with Fox for six months at 'the usual starlet salary' of $75 per week.[76] When she showed the contract to Grace, her legal guardian, and told her that as an actress her new name would be Marilyn 'as suggested by Mr. Lyon', Grace replied: 'Sounds fine for a first name. Why not use your mother's maiden name Monroe for your last name?'

To this, Marilyn agreed.[77] She now moved into the Hollywood Studio Club, Hollywood, 'a low-cost club for struggling models and aspiring actresses'.[78] She said: 'For the first six months I worked very hard, attending classes in acting, pantomime, singing, voice, and dancing'.[79]

In that summer of 1946, said Berniece, her mother Gladys 'continued working, and after a time she began doing assignments as a practical nurse'. In late summer, Gladys returned to Oregon.[80]

Dougherty reluctantly signed the divorce papers and delivered them to Marilyn. Subsequently, and not to his credit, he paraded his new lady friend in front of her. He now left for an eight-month assignment in the Far East.[81]

The divorce was finalised on 13 September 1946. Finally, Dougherty met Marilyn one last time for dinner.[82] Said Berniece: 'Marilyn sailed through the door on September 13 and gave me a bear hug and squealed "I'm a free woman again! Oh, I feel like celebrating!"'[83] Subsequently, said Berniece, Marilyn spoke 'frequently of Jim Dougherty, and with affection. She seems to feel no malice in the divorce action; they have simply grown to have opposing lifestyles'.[84]

In 1949, James Dougherty joined the Los Angeles Police Department (LAPD).[85]

## Subsequent Comments by Dougherty

Had it not been for the Second World War, he said regretfully, '[his] first marriage would have been [his] only one, and Norma Jean[e] Dougherty, a not-so-obscure housewife, would be living in retirement on the Arizona Desert today'.[86]

Following their divorce, Dougherty noticed some pictures of Marilyn in magazines. 'They had bleached out her hair and she even had a new way of smiling'.[87]

> I don't think that Norma Jean[e] ever really intended to become a sex symbol; when she entered films, she wanted to be an actress, someone who could play any part.[88]

When Marilyn did become an actress, Dougherty said:

> … peace and tranquillity, security, the uncomplicated joy of just being alive—all those things, I believe, went out of the window.[89]
>
> She just couldn't be Mrs Dougherty. She needed the divorce so she could get her movie contract. Someone had told her that Metro [Metro-Goldwyn-Mayer— MGM] almost never took on a starlet for the intensive training program that hopefully would lead to stardom if the girl was married. She might get pregnant and their investment would be lost.[90]
>
> That band continued to stretch and she got farther and farther away from the person she really wanted to be. I'm certain that always troubled her.[91]

Despite his sadness, Dougherty bore no grudge against Marilyn, and to his credit, he was generous in his remarks about his former wife: 'While Norma Jean had some serious faults … she retained within herself a kind of purity of spirit even as Marilyn. She was a beautiful person'.[92]

Also, having subsequently 'seen nearly all of her movies on television', he said, 'I began to see that she was a tremendous comedienne'.[94] Finally, said Dougherty, 'I have never stopped loving Norma Jean[e]'.[93]

# James Dougherty's Observations about Marilyn

James Dougherty's book, *The Secret Happiness of Marilyn Monroe*, was published in 1976. It contained many insightful remarks about Marilyn.

*Marilyn's Childhood*
Marilyn's mother, Gladys, said Dougherty, 'always saw that she was decently dressed'.[1]

*Her Possessiveness and Insecurity*
Marilyn, said Dougherty, 'wanted to be with me all the time'.[2] On their wedding day, 19 June 1942, he said:

> Except to go to the bathroom, she never let go of my arm all afternoon, and even then she looked at me as though she was afraid I might disappear while she was out of the room.[3]

Referring to spring 1942, said Dougherty: 'With the Goddards gone and Gladys in an institution, she really had no one except me and Aunt Ana'.[4]
The night before Dougherty joined the Merchant Marine, in late 1943, he stated:

> [Marilyn] had thrown herself frantically at me, begging me to make her pregnant so that she 'would have a piece of me, in case something happened'. She seemed to fear, now that she had me and her life had a direction for the first time, that it would end suddenly, that she would be cheated again by life the way she had been so many times before.[5]

The following day, he said, '[Marilyn] was almost in hysterics. If I hadn't had the foresight to move her in with Mom, I'm absolutely certain I could not have left her. Certainly not on her own.'[6] Dougherty's father, Edward, was currently absent in Thousand Oaks.

> There were frequent phone calls, long ones, during the five weeks of my basic training.[7]
>
> I know that she considered my shipping out and leaving Catalina as another rejection. In her rational mind, she knew I had to go, but she wasn't rational about such things. She was emotional.[8]
>
> She was always concerned about what people said or thought about her. If someone didn't like her or criticized her, it disturbed her terribly, because she didn't know how to hate back, not then anyway.[9]

When Dougherty's leave came to an end, and he returned to the ship, he stated:

> … that hit her extremely hard. She wanted something, *someone* that she could hold onto all the time. If we were out together, even at the movies, she had a tight grip on my arm or my hand.[10]

## Her Temperament

Marilyn was a Gemini, said Dougherty: 'There were moods in her that were unpredictable and often a little scary. You'd catch glimpses of someone who had been unloved for too long, unwanted too many years'.[11]

Yet on the positive side, Marilyn loved to sing: 'She had a cute little voice, kind of soft, not much volume. But it was sweet. And she always sang on key which is important'. Her favourite songs were '(I'll Be with You) In Apple Blossom Time' and 'When You Wish Upon a Star'.[12]

Marilyn liked it when he played the guitar, said Dougherty, and they sang 'a tearful ballad or two. She liked sentimental love songs: one in particular, "Tears On My Pillow"'.[13]

## Her Attitude to Childbearing

Dougherty explained to Marilyn that she would have 'a tough problem raising a child, as young as she was herself and working to support it. That child might end up like she did, with a mother who couldn't support it because of the pressures, and it would wind up in an institution. But she didn't agree, and she cried and wept all night'.[14]

He admitted that Marilyn 'had been talked out of having a family too soon by her husband [i.e. himself]'.[15] In other words, he felt that it was better to wait, presumably until the couple were more financially secure.

## Her Physicality

On their wedding day, said Dougherty, 'I knew I had to be careful that first night, that I was with a virgin', and he discounted 'the lurid tale, allegedly told by

Marilyn herself much, much later, that she had been raped at the age of eleven or twelve' as something that 'simply could not have happened'—in fact, it is by no means certain that Marilyn ever made such a claim. Nevertheless, said Dougherty, 'the myth continues that she was raped in one of the series of foster homes'.[16]

Dougherty stated: 'Norma Jean[e] loved sex. It was as natural to her as breakfast in the morning. There were never any problems with it'.[17] Her lovemaking was 'pure joy. Making love for Norma Jean was just another way of giving'.[18]

## Trustfulness

Dougherty described how Marilyn 'trusted everybody. She especially trusted [his] family and they took the place of the one she had always lacked'.[19]

## Domesticity

Marilyn liked to cook, said Dougherty: 'She was a fairly good one, especially if she followed a cookbook carefully'.[20]

## Attire, and Desire to be Physically Attractive

Dougherty described how Marilyn's 'drawn-out getting-ready ritual, had begun soon after we were married'.[21]

> [Although] she had no awareness that she was beautiful.... She *wanted* to be. She would rinse her face as many as fifteen times because she wanted a perfect complexion. If anything, she was too critical of herself.[22]
>
> Norma Jean[e] wore white a lot—an immaculate white dress or white slacks or shorts with a white blouse. She had the *cleanest* kind of beauty I've ever seen. And she wore a ribbon in her hair quite often, which added a touch of colour.[23]

## Disingenuousness about her Background: The 'Poor Little Orphan' Narrative

Dougherty stated that he himself came from a poor family:

> [Yet Marilyn had] never known grinding poverty, never had gone shoeless, never, to the best of my knowledge, had to skip a meal. I began to get the feeling that she desperately wanted some colourful family tale of want and scarcity, something that would clearly put her on the wrong side of the track so she could brag about it.[24]

However, there was another reason why Marilyn perpetrated the 'orphan' myth. Dougherty said:

For as long as she could manage, she told everyone that she was an orphan, not because she felt ashamed over her mother being confined to a state institution but because she knew the same thing would happen to Gladys that happened to me. Reporters would beat a path to her door, even in the hospital if they could manage it.[25]

### Honesty: Fidelity

Dougherty paid Marilyn this compliment. 'In all the years I was close to her, I never knew Norma Jean to lie.... [Furthermore] I know in my heart that she was never unfaithful, and ... I know that she didn't go the route of the casting couch to make her way up the ladder.[26, 27]

In other words, Marilyn did not prostitute herself in order to achieve success.

### A Desire to be Liked

Dougherty said:

[Marilyn] wanted to be liked because she'd been parcelled out just so much love—not enough, perhaps—from each foster home she'd lived in. And I'm sure in time, when she was out on her own and no longer had my shoulder to lean on, she wanted love from fans, from audiences, maybe from the whole damn world. But that's a pretty frail substitute for the real thing and I'm sure she found that out. She wasn't easily fooled.[28]

Dougherty did not become embittered, even though Marilyn had given him some cause to be so: for example, by sending him his divorce papers when he was thousands of miles away on active service rather than discussing it with him face to face. He also saw the good side of her, and it is therefore likely that his account of her is truthful.

# Early Success,
# Popularity, and a Scandal

In September 1946, Marilyn told Berniece that she had 'posed nude for a photographer': 'I'm not ashamed. I did it. And that's that. But I don't want Aunt Ana to know. She wouldn't approve'.[1]

Throughout 1947, Marilyn attended the Actors Laboratory, Crescent Heights Boulevard, West Hollywood, LA, where aspiring playwrights, actors, and producers showcased their work. Here she was tutored by US stage and film actor Morris Carnovsky, and by his wife, US actress Phoebe Brand.

In February 1947, Fox renewed Marilyn's contract and doubled her salary to $150 per week. Said she: 'I was so excited, I went out and bought five hundred dollars' worth of clothes'.[2] In the same month, the filming of *Scudda-Hoo! Scudda-Hay!* (in which Marilyn was cast) commenced. However, she was scathing about the tiny role that Fox had given her in the film, and declared that this was the smallest part she ever had.

> If you watched the movie real close during the dancing, you would see a sixty-second close-up of my back during one of those dancing numbers. I guess the studio didn't think enough of my back scene, and the next time my contract option came up they let me go. It was August 1947. What a blow to my ego. What a blow to my career.[3]

Were the words of the film's title, '*Scudda-Hoo! Scudda-Hay!*', all that she was required to say, she was asked? Smiling charmingly, she replied with a mixture of ruefulness and sarcasm: 'No. In the picture ... I had one word to say. I said "Hello". But it went fast. In fact they cut it out'.[4]

Marilyn's first film, in which she played a very minor role, was *Dangerous Years* (Fox, released December 1947), starring Billy Halop, Ann E. Todd, and Scotty Beckett.

It was through the efforts of Whitey Snyder—who in August 1947 became Marilyn's favourite make-up artist—and others that Marilyn's features were transformed into the iconic image that became instantly recognisable for throughout the world.

On 25 August 1947, Fox chose not to renew Marilyn's contract, and she now returned to the Hollywood Studio Club.[5] In order to pay her rent etc., she recommended modelling. 'Now that I had to pay for my acting lessons, I often went without eating', she said.[6] Nevertheless, Berniece said, 'Marilyn told me she was able to keep up her determination through Aunt Ana's love and encouragement'[7] Marilyn rejected the idea of taking a lover in order to improve her financial situation.

> Respect is one of life's greatest treasures. I mean, what does this all add up to if you don't have that? If there [is] only one thing in my life I [am] proud of, it's that I've never been a kept women.[8]

In October 1947, Marilyn was cast in a stage production of *Glamour Preferred* at the Bliss-Hayden Miniature Theater, Beverly Hills.[9]

According to George Barris, Joseph 'Joe' M. Schenck, co-founder and chairman of Twentieth Century Fox Studios, became Marilyn's 'close friend and benefactor. Although word had it that Marilyn was the mistress of the long-married but frequently faithless Schenck, she always denied it'.

It was Schenck who pleaded with Fox to renew Marilyn's contract, and when the company refused, he 'persuaded his friend Harry Cohn, head of Columbia Pictures, to sign Marilyn'.[10]

On 9 March 1948, said Marilyn:

> On the strength of a screen test I had made at Fox, Columbia Pictures hired me at the usual starlet salary being paid then—one hundred twenty-five dollars a week. Boy—was I in heaven. They had me study with the studio's drama coach, Natasha Lytess. She was the first person of authority I met who believed I could make a fine actress if I worked hard at it.[11]

On 14 March 1948, to Marilyn's deep regret, Ana Lower died at the age of sixty-eight.[12]

In late April 1948, Marilyn prepared for a forthcoming singing role in *Ladies of the Chorus* (Columbia 1948), under Columbia's vocal coach, Fred Karger. The two became friends, then lovers. At one time, she pleaded with him to marry her, but he refused, telling her she would not be a suitable mother for his daughter from a previous marriage because she was too wrapped up in her career. Heartbroken, she remained friends with 'Freddy' and with his family. The couple continued to date on and off.[13] It was Karger who arranged for Marilyn to have dental treatment to straighten her front teeth.[14]

On 8 September 1948, Columbia failed to renew Marilyn's contract with the company, at which decision she was 'shocked', she said.[15]

From 16 November 1948 and for a period of three years, photographer and artist Earl Moran converted photographs that he had taken of Marilyn into 'pin-up' posters.

On New Year's Eve 1948, at a party given by producer Sam Spiegel, Marilyn was introduced to Russo-American talent agent Johnny Hyde, Executive Vice-President of Hollywood's William Morris (talent) Agency. He was aged fifty-three and she twenty-two, and for him, it was love at first sight. However, he was not in good health.

In spring 1949, Hyde made Marilyn an offer of marriage. This she declined, on the grounds that whereas she loved him, she was not in love with him. Nevertheless, Hyde engineered another minor role for Marilyn in *All About Eve*.

At about that time, said Berniece, 'mother sent us a photograph of her new "husband" John Stewart Eley'.[16] However, some months later, Gladys discovered that Eley 'already had a wife in Idaho'.[17]

Marilyn was currently residing at the Hollywood Studio Club. She 'was really broke' she said, when on 27 May 1949, she approached photographer Tom Kelley at his photographic studio—736 North Seward Avenue, Hollywood—and offered to pose in the nude for him.[18] He agreed, for a fee payable to Marilyn of a mere $50.

Kelley's iconic portrait of Marilyn, entitled 'Golden Dreams', subsequently appeared on calendars produced by the Tom Kelley Studio, as did other photographs of her by Kelley, including 'A New Wrinkle'.

In September 1949, Marilyn had a brief affair with the aforementioned photographer Milton H. Greene.[19]

On 11 May 1950, Hyde negotiated a seven-year contract for Marilyn at Fox, for a salary of $500 a week. Subsequently, in October 1950, with Hyde's support, Marilyn signed a new contract with Fox for a salary of $750 a week—'ten times the amount she had made as a starlet when she was let go from Fox three years before'.[20]

In that autumn of 1950, for reasons of economy, Marilyn agreed to move in with Natasha Lytess who lived at an apartment at 1309 North Harper Avenue, LA, with her daughter, Barbara. Said Ezra Goodman, Natasha 'was not only Monroe's dramatic coach but friend, adviser and general guide'.[21]

In that same autumn of 1950, Marilyn attended classes on literature and the history of art at the University College of Los Angeles (UCLA) for a period of ten weeks.

Hyde's health was now beginning to fail. However, on 5 December 1950, he secured a contract for Marilyn with the William Morris Agency. He died on 18 December 1950, aged fifty-five. Goodman related how Natasha Lytess had told him how, 'some years ago' (it was late December 1950), 'Monroe and she drove out to a Southern California community because

Monroe wanted to try to see her father, whom she had never met. 'We went to this farm,' said Lytess. 'Marilyn tried to contact him from the area. She called him three times and finally got through to him. He refused to see her. His voice sounded cold and cruel. He said, 'I have a family and children'. He took her phone number and said he'd contact her in Los Angeles and never did'.

Lytess said Monroe had known about her father for a long time before she had finally worked up the courage to try to see him.[22]

In January 1951, when Natasha Lytess's lease expired, Marilyn moved into the Beverly Carlton Hotel.

On 11 May 1951, Marilyn signed a new contract with Fox for a seven-year period at a salary of $500 per week 'with semi-annual raises'. Said she:

> It was my fans who wanted me, who made me a star. The studio was finally doing something about it because of the pressure that came from the public. Orders were issued by Mr. Zanuck to all producers to find a part for me in their films.[23]

In that spring of 1951, Marilyn stated:

> [Roy Croft in the Publicity Department at Fox] got a bright idea. He was going to build me up as a pin-up, a sex queen. That really did the trick. Editors around the world began publishing my pin-up pictures. The studio said I was receiving more mail for photo requests than their biggest star, Betty Grable.[24]

By now, said Berniece, Marilyn 'felt like she was getting somewhere. But she yearned for more varied roles'.[25]

In autumn 1951, Marilyn commenced drama classes with actor and acting coach Michael Chekhov, nephew of Russian dramatist Anton Chekhov, and a former student of Russian theatre practitioner Constantin Stanislavski.

In her notebook, *circa* 1951, Marilyn stated as follows:

> Fear of giving me the lines new
> maybe won't be able to learn them
> maybe I'll make mistakes
> people will either think I'm no good or
> laugh or belittle me or think I can't act.
> Women looked stern and critical—
> unfriendly and cold in general
> afraid director won't think I'm any good.
> remembering when I couldn't do a god
> damn thing.[26]

In fact, Marilyn always had problems remembering her lines, which is why she could never have achieved success on the stage.

In December 1951, Marilyn moved in with Natasha Lytess at her new house, 611 North Crescent Drive, West Hollywood.

In March 1952, Berniece's husband, Paris Miracle, returned from work with 'a roll of a dozen calendars under his arm'. They featured studies of Marilyn in the nude.[27] The explanation for this is as follows.

One of the nude photographs of Marilyn, taken by Tom Kelley in May 1949 and dubbed 'Golden Dreams', was sold to John Baumgarth, and in 1952 (and from 1953 to 1955), it featured in a calendar produced by the Baumgarth Calendar Company. The photograph was also reproduced on posters throughout the land.

During the furore that ensued, Marilyn remained unperturbed, and when a reporter asked her, in respect of the calendar, if she had had anything on during the filming—the answer to which, of course, was obvious—she replied, wittily, 'only the radio'.[28]

However, for Marilyn, there was a price to pay. James Dougherty said:

[The] stretching of the band that was between Norma Jean[e], who had enormous self respect, and Marilyn [came when] she had to separate the two—to earn a living in the movies or in modelling, as with the nude calendar.[29]

On 7 April 1952, Marilyn's image appeared on the front cover of *Life* magazine.

John Eley died on 23 April 1952, by which time Gladys, who was currently jobless, had left him and moved in with Grace Goddard.

On 28 April 1952, Marilyn underwent an appendicectomy at the Cedars of Lebanon Hospital, LA. While she was convalescing, she learned that certain facts about her were shortly to be revealed in the media. George Carpozi described how it was Erskine Johnson, NEA's (Newspaper Enterprise Associations) Hollywood correspondent, who had 'gotten a tip that Marilyn's stories about her early childhood were not historically correct [i.e.] that she was an orphan: that she had never seen her mother or father. Erskine Johnson somehow had an intuition about a particular patient in the state hospital who had been raving that Marilyn Monroe was her daughter'.

Johnson duly tracked down Marilyn's mother, Gladys, and told the authorities at Twentieth Century Fox of his discovery.[30] Berniece said: '[The] story broke ... that Marilyn was not an orphan after all. [Whereupon] Marilyn admitted that this was true'.[31]

In the summer of 1952, Gladys stayed with Berniece and Paris Miracle, who had relocated to Florida in 1948.[32] As for Marilyn, she told Berniece that she and Gladys 'could never live together':

... I thought maybe it was just me—just the clash of our personalities—but perhaps, unfortunately, she just isn't cut out to live with anyone. Let's get Mother into an apartment of her own and see if that will work. Can we try it?[33]

Gladys, however, refused to countenance the idea, and after seven weeks, 'Marilyn directs Grace to mail Gladys a ticket to come back to Los Angeles by train.'[34] Said Berniece:

When mother got back to California, she went straight to Grace and Doc's house [in L.A.]. She started screaming on the front porch about Grace sending a train ticket instead of a plane ticket. Grace said Mother stood there in a rage yelling at them without stopping.[35]

The outcome was that in November 1952, Grace arranged for Gladys 'after seven years of freedom', to be admitted to Norwalk State Hospital for The Mentally Ill, Norwalk, LA.

In December 1952, a nude photograph of Marilyn appeared on the front cover of the first-ever issue of *Playboy* magazine. Other magazines that carried photographs of her included *Modern Screen, Screen Annual, Look, Cosmopolitan, Movieland*, and *Screen Life*.

On 9 February 1953, Marilyn was presented with *Photoplay* magazine's Gold Medal Award as 'the selection of all the movie-goers of America who have voted you the most popular actress of the year.'[36] When US film and television actress Joan Crawford criticised the way that Marilyn had presented herself at the award ceremony, i.e. by wearing a low-cut dress, Marilyn responded in her usual charming way, deflecting the criticism by praising 'Miss Crawford' for 'being such a wonderful mother' and for giving those children whom she had adopted, in addition to her own, 'a fine home'.

On that same day, 9 February 1953, at Marilyn's request, Gladys was transferred to Rockhaven Sanitarium (a private mental institution for women at what is now the city of Glendale, 8 miles north of LA, which opened in 1923).[37] Said Berniece: 'Marilyn moved mother to Rockhaven when her career began to climb and she could afford the expense.'[38]

In summer 1953, Milton Greene photographed Marilyn for *Look* magazine, for which he was currently working. Said Goodman: 'Monroe was enchanted with Greene's photographic approach.'[39]

When Grace Goddard died on 28 September 1953, aged fifty-nine, Marilyn told Berniece: 'I feel an anchor is gone. Life is just one loss after another. What will I do without her?' Although Doc told Marilyn and Berniece that Grace had died of cancer, Berniece subsequently discovered from Grace's death certificate that she had actually committed suicide 'by means of barbiturate poisoning; ingestion of phenobarbital'.[40] Was Marilyn's friend, baseball star Joe DiMaggio, of some comfort to her, Berniece enquired. 'I guess he's more important than ever to me now,' Marilyn replied.[41]

On 4 January 1954, Marilyn was suspended by Fox for walking out of a production of *Pink Tights*, in which she co-starred with Frank Sinatra. Said Berniece:

> … she objects to the script, to her lack of director approval, and her salary. She wants a voice in choosing the roles in which she is cast. She feels that the role in *Pink Tights* is not only a demeaning characterization but also poorly written.[42]

Furthermore, the film was 'a remake of an old Betty Grable film'.[43] Soon afterwards, Marilyn was reinstated by Fox, but on 26 January, she was suspended once again.

Films in which Marilyn featured between 1947 and 1954 were as follows:

## *Ladies of the Chorus*
Columbia, December 1948
Starring Adele Jergens, Marilyn Monroe, and Rand Brooks.

Marilyn's role in the film, she said, 'was that of a strip-teaser in a burlesque show. I got to sing and dance, but … the film did not create any excitement'.[44] However, she played her part with poise and grace and, as always, with her trademark radiant smile.

## *Love Happy*
United Artists, October 1949
Starring Harpo Marx, Chico Marx, Groucho Marx, Ilona Massey, Vera-Ellen, Marion Hutton, and Marilyn Monroe.

It was an actress whom Marilyn happened to meet by chance, while having lunch at a restaurant, who suggested that she try for a part in a Marx Brothers film. The RKO Studio (RKO Pictures Inc., a US film production and distribution company), said the actress, was looking for a blonde, and the film was entitled *Love Happy*. Marilyn duly telephoned the producer, Lester Cowan.[45]

This was for a walk-on role, lasting for one minute, and with minimal speaking lines. Despite this, said Marilyn, Cowan 'made [her] a star of that film even though [she] had only one scene and one line'.[46] The scene in question was when private detective Sam Grunion (Groucho Marx) says to his client (Marilyn), 'Is there anything I can do for you', and she replies, 'Mr Grunion, I want you to help me. Some men are following me'. 'Really? I can't understand why!' Yet Sam's expression belies his words, as he peers after her, rolling his eyes lasciviously.

Said Berniece, Marilyn stole the show even though she only played the part of 'an anonymous pedestrian'.[47] Following the release of *Love Happy*, said Marilyn: 'I was sent to some of the larger cities in the country on a personal appearance tour for five weeks'.[48]

There now followed press interviews, television and radio appearances, and newspaper publicity. During the promotional tour, Marilyn was famously photographed on Jones Beach, New York State, by her 'photographer friend, André de Dienes'.[49]

Having seen the film *Love Happy*, Johnny Hyde sought Marilyn out and arranged for her to appear in a TV commercial advertising a motor car, and in *The Fireball* (Fox, November 1950), a low-budget movie starring Mickey Rooney and Pat O'Brien. Hyde also paid for her to have plastic surgery to shorten the tip of her somewhat retroussé nose.

## The Asphalt Jungle
MGM, May 1950
Starring Sterling Hayden, Louis Calhern, Jean Hagen, James Whitmore, Sam Jaffe, and John McIntire.

It was through Johnny Hyde that his friend, film director John Huston, arranged for Marilyn to audition for a part in a forthcoming film: *The Asphalt Jungle*. Huston described her reading as 'extraordinarily good. She was ideal. She was the girl. However [he] had no notion that she was going to go on and become the star which she became'.[50]

At MGM, director of the Talent Department Lucille Ryman, told Marilyn that she 'had talent as an actress', and also that she could 'count on her as a friend'.[51] On 25 August 1947, Lucille and her husband, actor John Carroll, invited Marilyn to share their apartment at La Cienega Boulevard, West Hollywood, rent free. Said Marilyn: 'I felt I had a guardian angel looking after me'.[52] The outcome was that she was offered a part in the film *The Asphalt Jungle*.

In the film, which was directed by John Huston, a recently released convict hatches a plot with a bookmaker and a high-profile lawyer Emmerich to steal jewellery worth $500,000. In the course of events, a private detective is murdered. Emmerich disposes of the body and creates an alibi for himself with the aid of his mistress, Angela (Marilyn). The police commissioner finally persuades Angela to tell the truth.

Marilyn is convincing in her part as one who is torn between being truthful, or being loyal to Uncle Emmerich. In fact, she considered this to be her best performance.[53] Nonetheless, she was perfectly well aware of how demeaning some of the film roles that had been assigned to her were, as she revealed in a letter to columnist Dorothy Kilgallen.[54] In *The Asphalt Jungle* she said: 'I played a vacuous, rich man's darling attempting to carry herself in a sophisticated manner'.

The *Asphalt Jungle* was billed as 'The hit that made Marilyn Monroe great'. Hyde subsequently found Marilyn parts in *Right Cross* (1950, MGM) and *Home Town Story* (1951, MGM).

## All About Eve
Fox, October 1950
Starring Bette Davis, Anne Baxter, George Sanders, and Celeste Holm.

On the strength of the part that she had played in *The Asphalt Jungle*, director and writer Joseph Mankiewicz offered Marilyn the part of Miss Casswell in the film *All About Eve*. Darryl Zanuck 'immediately offered me a contract', said Marilyn. However, it transpired that 'Miss Casswell was a dumb blonde', and 'the part was a small one'.[55] The film depicts a rivalry between an ageing film star and her ambitious admirer, who threatens both her career and her personal relationships.

Marilyn described her role in the film, which was extremely minor, as that of 'an untalented showgirl'.[56] However, Barris described *All About Eve* as 'one of Hollywood's finest films ever' and he stated that Marilyn played the 'small part' of Miss Casswell—'a girl who would do anything to get ahead'—'beautifully'.[57]

## Clash by Night
RKO, June 1952
Starring Barbara Stanwyck, Paul Douglas, Robert Ryan, Marilyn Monroe, and Keith Andes.

It was Sidney Skolsky, a New York press agent and one of Marilyn's 'trusted' and 'loyal friends', who persuaded RKO producer Jerry Wald to offer her the part of 'a sex-wild girl named Peggy' in his next film, *Clash By Night*. Incidentally, RKO was the film company for whom Marilyn's mother, Gladys, had previously worked. Said Barris, Marilyn's attachment to Skolsky 'became so strong [that she] would not sign a contract or take part in a movie unless she first spoke with Sidney about it'.[58]

## Don't Bother to Knock
Fox, July 1952
Starring Richard Widmark and Marilyn Monroe.

Nell (Marilyn) babysits for a couple in a New York hotel, in which she pretends to be a guest. However, an airline pilot, who is one of the guests, becomes suspicious of her behaviour. Nell is, in fact, the niece of the hotel's lift operator, Eddie.

When the little girl Bunny is discovered having been bound and gagged by her babysitter, Nell, Eddie reveals that the latter, having attempted suicide, has spent the previous three years in a psychiatric hospital. As the net closes in on Nell, she holds a razor to her throat. This is ironic, given the fact that the real-life Marilyn made several attempts at suicide, as will be seen.

Marilyn, who was billed in the film *Don't Bother to Knock* as 'America's most exciting personality', described how, as Nell, she played the part of 'an emotionally unstable, unfortunate girl driven to attempted homicide by fear'.[59, 60] In doing so, her body language, facial expressions, and intonations created just the amount of drama and suspense that was required.

## Monkey Business
Fox, September 1952
Starring Cary Grant, Ginger Rogers, Marilyn Monroe, and James Coburn.

A research chemist attempts to discover the elixir of youth. When he himself drinks the potion that he and one of his experimental chimpanzees has concocted, he becomes rejuvenated and childlike. When both his wife and his secretary, Lois Laurel (Marilyn), also drink it, inadvertently, hilarity ensues.

Portrayed as an incompetent typist, Marilyn enters into the spirit of this witty and amusing film, but once again, she only plays a minor role. In this 'light comedy' said Marilyn, 'I played a slightly dumb secretary who couldn't type.'[61]

Marilyn made the following note about the part of Lois, whom she played in the film ('Oxley' being Oliver Oxley, played by Charles Coburn).

> Oh yes Mr. Oxley is always
> complaining about my punctuation
> so I'm careful to get here
> before 9:00.[62]

When Marilyn wrote 'punctuation', what she meant was 'punctuality'. In fact, Marilyn was notorious for her own, real-life unpunctuality.

## Niagara
Fox, January 1953
Starring Marilyn Monroe, Joseph Cotton, Jean Peters, and Max Showalter.

A honeymoon couple visit Niagara Falls and meet George and his wife, Rose (Marilyn), who was billed as 'the tantalizing temptress whose kisses fired men's souls!' Patrick, Rose's lover, plans to murder George, but the plan misfires and it is George who kills Patrick.

Filmed in colour, against the dramatic backdrop of Niagara Falls, Rose wears highly luminescent, ruby-red lipstick, and upstages all the other female guests at the hotel with her highly revealing, pink, low-cut dress. *Niagara* was one of the few films of the time to be made in Technicolor.

In *Niagara*, said Marilyn, 'the girl I played … was an amoral type whose plot to kill her husband was attempted with no apparent cost to her conscience.'[63]

Said actor Robert Cornthwaite, who played the part of Dr Zoldeck in the film:

[Marilyn] was being courted at the time by Joe DiMaggio, who was around [the film set], and when he wasn't there Marilyn would get on the phone to him. She would continue her conversation while the tape was going on, and the assistant would come to her and say 'Honey! Get off the phone! We're shooting!', and she would just look at her with those big eyes and go right on talking.[64]

## Gentlemen Prefer Blondes
Fox, July 1953
Starring Jane Russell and Marilyn Monroe.

Two glamorous showgirls, one of whom is called Lorelei Lee (Marilyn), seek wealthy husbands as they set sail aboard a luxury liner for France.

Marilyn plays the part of an obsequious, dumb blonde with an affected voice, who engages in vacuous conversations and seems primarily interested in jewellery. However, there is an amusing incident when Lorelei says that she does not intend to marry her fiancée Mr Esmond Jr, for his money but for his father Mr Esmond Sr's money.

Said Marilyn: 'I played the Lorelei Lee role. Her preoccupation with diamonds was a harmless enough interest.'[65]

The film was billed as 'the most glamorous musical of our age' and Marilyn gave a memorable rendition of the song, 'Diamonds are a Girl's Best Friend'.

> Men grow cold as girls grow old
> And we all lose our charms in the end
> But square cut or pear shaped
> These rocks don't lose their shape
> Diamonds are a girl's best friend.

## How to Marry a Millionaire
Fox, November 1953
Starring Marilyn Monroe, Betty Grable, Lauren Bacall, and William Powell.

Pola (Marilyn), who has poor eyesight and wears spectacles throughout, and two other 'gold digging' ladies rent a luxury penthouse in New York City. Their landlord is Freddie, a tax exile who lives in Europe.

Pola falls for a wealthy, but crooked speculator who she hopes will take her to Arabia and shower jewellery upon her. She plans to meet him in Kansas City. However, owing to her poor eyesight, she boards the wrong aeroplane, only to discover that sitting next to her is Freddie, a relative pauper, with whom she falls in love.

With her simpering voice and mannerisms, Pola is the perfect foil for Loco (Betty Grable), who gives a magisterial performance as 'senior partner' of the three, and who describes her two lady colleagues as 'those bubble heads'.

The film was produced by Fox in 'Cinemascope' (i.e. widescreen format). Said Derek Malcolm, film critic, *London Evening Standard*:

> It's only a minor film, but the playing was very, very good, and very witty and very sophisticated. But the one who sort of comes out beyond Bacall and Grable is Marilyn, in her glasses, so short-sighted that she can't even find the millionaire let alone marry him. And, you know, everybody thought she was wonderful.[66]

Other films in which Marilyn featured between 1947 and 1953 were *Dangerous Years* (Fox, 1947); *A Ticket to Tomahawk* (Fox, 1950); *The Fireball* (Fox, 1950); *Right Cross* (M.G.M., 1950); *Home Town Story* (M.G.M., 1951); *As Young as You Feel* (Fox, 1951); *Love Nest* (Fox, 1951); *Let's Make It Legal* (Fox, 1951); *We're Not Married* (Fox, 1952); and *O. Henry's Full House* (Fox, 1952).[67]

Of Marilyn's film roles, Berniece made the following insightful comments:

> Most people thought that Marilyn was playing herself in roles like she had in *Show Business* [released 16 December 1954], *Monkey Business*, or *Gentlemen Prefer Blondes*. Viewers based this opinion on the seeming lack of skill that her roles required, and upon the similarity between these characters and the public image she projected during the first half of her career. However, most of the roles that were given to Marilyn were the opposite of her personality. Marilyn was not a dumb blond.[68]

# Second Marriage:
# Joe DiMaggio

Marilyn's career was now 'blossoming with starring roles', said Berniece, referring to the year 1952. Furthermore, 'a romance is blossoming with Joe DiMaggio'.[1]

Joseph 'Joe' Paul DiMaggio was born on 25 November 1914 in Martinez, California, to Sicilian immigrants Guiseppe, a fisherman, and Rosalia (*née* Mercurio). During the Second World War, DiMaggio served with the US Army Air Forces. On 19 November 1939, he married actress Dorothy Arnold, who bore him a son, Joseph (junior, born 23 October 1941). The couple divorced in 1944.

On 11 December 1951, at the age of thirty-seven, the legendary star retired from playing professional baseball with the New York Yankees—after a fifteen-year career.

Marilyn first met DiMaggio, who was eleven years her senior, in the spring of 1952. He had expressed a desire to meet her to a friend of his, who had arranged a rendezvous for the pair at a restaurant in Sunset Boulevard, West Hollywood. Marilyn subsequently remarked to Berniece's daughter, Mona Rae: 'He's the only man in my life. I love him very much'.[2] The couple were married in San Francisco on 14 January 1954.

Marilyn and DiMaggio commenced married life in 'a lovely cottage in Beverly Hills'. Said George Barris:

> When Marilyn married Joe DiMaggio, she was in love not only with him, but with his large and loving family, too. She probably found in them, as in the families of other friends and lovers, a replacement for the whole family she had so needed as a young girl.[3]

On 1 February 1954, the couple flew to Japan so that DiMaggio could fulfil a commitment to put in an appearance at the start of that country's baseball season. On 9 February, Marilyn flew on to Korea, where she visited US troops stationed there, and delighted them by singing 'Diamonds are a Girl's Best

Friend'—wiggling her hips; blowing them kisses; and delivering witticisms such as: 'I don't know why you boys are always getting so excited about sweater girls. Take away the sweaters and what have you got?'[4]

The Korean War, fought between North and South Korea, had commenced on 25 June 1950 and ended on 27 July 1953.

On 13 April 1954, Fox reinstated Marilyn. Soon, however, she declared: 'Joe started complaining about my working all the time. It got so that we didn't even talk to each other for days'.[5] Said Barris:

> Marilyn's storybook marriage to the American sport's icon Joe DiMaggio was doomed from the start; her career demanded that she remain in the public eye; he was through with all that, never liked it much in the first place, and considered himself well out of the limelight. He wanted to settle down and make a home. Although Marilyn, too, was basically a private person, her career was going into overdrive, and there were more and more invitations and appearances that she couldn't afford to turn down if she wanted her fortunes to continue to rise.[6]

In August 1954, on the set of *There's No Business Like Show Business*, Marilyn met Paula Strasberg, who invited her to visit the Actors Studio, New York, where her husband, Lee Strasberg, was director and teacher of drama.

In autumn 1954, said Arthur Miller:

> Marilyn was absenting herself from Hollywood in an all but acknowledged strike until her business partner, the photographer Milton Greene, could renegotiate her Twentieth Century Fox contract so she could periodically make independent pictures with her own [proposed] new company [to be called] Marilyn Monroe Productions.[7]

Interviewed by the press at the home of Greene and his wife, Amy, in Weston, Connecticut, Marilyn was asked whether she was now tired of playing the same type of roles all the time. She replied, smiling charmingly: 'It's not that I object to doing musicals or comedies. In fact, I rather enjoy it, but I would like to do dramatic parts too'. Nonetheless, she looked drawn and strained.[8]

On 14 September 1954, during the filming of *The Seven Year Itch*, Marilyn described a particular scene in which she stood above a grating in Lexington Avenue, Manhattan, New York City, while an air-blowing machine mimicked the effect of an underground train passing underneath.

> This sent my dress flying waist high, revealing my legs and white panties. A crowd had gathered even though it was two or three in the morning. They consisted of men who somehow had heard about our late night filming. Among the crowd was my husband Joe. When Billy Wilder [Austrian-born Jewish-American filmmaker,

and the film's director] kept shooting the scene over and over, [and] the crowd of men kept on applauding and shouting 'more, more, Marilyn—let's see more', Joe became upset.[9]

For her husband DiMaggio, said Marilyn, her 'dress-flying scene' for the film *The Seven Year Itch*, 'my exposing my legs and thighs, even my crotch—that was the last straw'.[10] Said Wilder, Joe 'didn't like it.'[11] In the event, this scene was never screened. Instead, it was reshot at the Hollywood Studio 'in a more refined way'.[12] At the 'wrap party'—held to celebrate the completion of shooting—Marilyn danced with her idol, Clark Gable.

DiMaggio now left for San Francisco. As for Marilyn, she travelled to New York where, with Milton Greene, she founded Marilyn Monroe Productions, with herself as president and Greene as vice-president and treasurer.[13]

In January 1955, Marilyn was 'finalizing arrangements' for the new company.[14] She had previously complained to Greene about the paltry remuneration that she received, and the equally paltry film roles to which she had been assigned. This would give her more control over her own destiny.

On 4 February 1955, Marilyn again visited the Actors Studio in New York, where she was introduced to its director, Lee Strasberg. It was in New York in the summer of 1955 that actor Eli Wallach took Marilyn to see a play. She had never seen a play before, he said, and when he took her backstage, she asked him, 'How do you do this? How do you do this thing on the stage?' Wallach told her that for two years he had been appearing, six times a week, in the play *The Teahouse of the August Moon*. Whereupon she enquired of him, 'do you think I could ever learn it?'[15]

At about that time, Lee Strasberg agreed for Marilyn to sit in on some acting classes. She now asked Strasberg if his wife, Paula, might help her; to which he also agreed.[16] The Strasbergs taught 'The Method' of acting. This, Berniece described as a process 'by which actors draw on their emotions and experiences to create realistic characterizations'.[17]

*The Seven Year Itch* premiered on 1 June 1955: an event that DiMaggio and Marilyn attended together. It was also Marilyn's twenty-ninth birthday.

In October 1955, Marilyn asked director Elia Kazan to cast her in the title role in the film *Baby Doll*, based on a play by Tennessee Williams. However, Kazan refused her request and the following lines, written by Marilyn, explain why:

> He [Kazan] said that
> I've become so deified
> as a sex symbol
> that [the] public [will] never except [i.e. accept] me as
> a virgin and as a nineteen/twenty year old.[18]

Marilyn was, in fact, aged twenty-nine at the time.

In that same month of October 1955, Fox came to an agreement with the Music Corporation of America (MCA), representing Marilyn, about a new contract. This would be for four films over seven years, with the option of acting in other films for herself or for other studios. Her retainer would be $100,000 a year.

As for her husband, said Marilyn:

> Joe admitted he still loved me, but my being a movie star was too much for him to take any longer. He became impossible to live with. I guess at the time there was nothing to do but get divorced.[19]

During her divorce proceedings, Marilyn's smile, for once, was missing. She looked sad and was unable to talk to the press. 'I'm sorry, I'm very sorry', she told them.[20] On 31 October 1955, Marilyn's divorce from DiMaggio was finalised.

Films in which Marilyn featured between 1954 and 1955 were as follows:

## River of No Return
Fox, April 1954
Starring Robert Mitchum, Marilyn Monroe, Tommy Rettig, and Rory Calhoun.

Matt (Robert Mitchum) is a widower who has recently served a term of imprisonment for murder. Meanwhile, his son, Mark, is left in the care of dance-hall singer Kay (Marilyn), whose fiancée is Harry (Rory Calhoun), a gambler. Kay and Matt journey together on a raft; brave rapids; and survive attacks by a mountain lion and by native Indian warriors.

A highlight of the film is when Marilyn sings the song 'River of No Return' quite beautifully. During the filming, however, said Marilyn, she almost drowned in the Bow River 'when the icy torrent dragged [her] downstream'.[21]

## There's No Business Like Show Business
Fox, December 1954
Starring Ethel Merman, Donald O'Connor, Marilyn Monroe, Dan Dailey, Johnnie Ray, and Mitzi Gaynor.

This is a musical featuring a family of singers, 'The Five Donahues'. At a nightclub, young Tim Donahue (Donald O'Connor) meets Victoria (Marilyn), a singer. The pair meet again in Miami, and Tim arranges for her to sing with the Donahues. After a misunderstanding, Tim disappears. Finally, the five Donahues are reunited.

A highlight of the film is Marilyn's rendition of the song 'Heat Wave' by Irving Berlin.

*The Seven Year Itch*
Fox, June 1955
Starring Marilyn Monroe and Tom Ewell.

The film is described as a 'scandalous, sexy comedy', and the action takes place during 'a steamy summer in New York City'.

With his wife and son away on holiday, publishing executive Richard (Tom Ewell), meets an actress (Marilyn, referred to as 'The Girl'), when she rents the apartment upstairs.

When he reads Chapter 3 of psychiatrist Dr Brubaker's book, entitled *The Repressed Urge of the Middle-Aged Male*, Richard fantasises that he himself is playing Rachmaninov's Second Piano Concerto while Marilyn, dressed up to the nines, is draped over the piano. He returns to his psychology book and discovers that he is suffering from what is described as 'The Seven Year Itch'.

Now comes the aforementioned famous—some might say infamous—scene where Marilyn stands over a grating and the breeze from the subway blows her skirt upwards. Marilyn enters into the spirit of the film, demonstrating once again that comedy is her forte.

# Third Marriage:
# Arthur Miller

US playwright and essayist Arthur Asher Miller was born on 17 October 1915 in Harlem, New York, to Isidore Miller, clothing manufacturer of Polish-Jewish descent and his wife, Augusta (*née* Barnett), of New York City. The stock market crash of 24 October 1929 adversely affected the Miller's business, and the family were obliged to relocate to the New York borough of Brooklyn.

Having attended Abraham Lincoln High School, where he developed an interest in literature, Miller studied journalism and English at the University of Michigan (majoring in 1936). In that year, he won the prestigious Avery Hopwood Award for playwriting. He subsequently joined the Federal Theater Project (1938–1940), a state sponsored programme designed to promote theatrical and other live entertainment throughout the US.

On 5 August 1940, Miller married his college sweetheart, Mary Grace Slattery, and the couple set up home at Willow Street, Brooklyn Heights, New York. She bore him two children, Jane and Robert. In that year, his first play to be performed, *The Man Who Had All the Luck*, was staged. During the Second World War, Miller worked as a ship fitter's assistant at the Brooklyn Naval Yard.

In winter 1947, Miller purchased a farmhouse in Welton Road, Roxbury, Connecticut, and the following year, he added a small studio, in which he wrote the first act of his play, *Death of a Salesman*. Two years later, in 1949, the play opened on Broadway, Manhattan, to great acclaim. For *Death of a Salesman*, Miller won the Pulitzer Prize Award for drama.

In his book *Timebends: A Life*, Miller described how he first met Marilyn in December 1950 in Hollywood 'on the set of a film in which she had a bit part—a movie starring Monty Woolley'.[1] This was a reference to *As Young as You Feel* (released 15 June 1951). Miller was a decade older than Marilyn, she being as yet, 'an unknown young actress'.[2] They had been introduced to each other by Miller's friend, the film and theatre director Elia Kazan. The two would not meet again for four years.[3]

In 1953, Miller's play *The Crucible* opened on Broadway. Ostensibly about the witch-hunts that took place in Salem Massachusetts between 1692 and 1693, the play was, in reality, an allegory that could be interpreted as a criticism of 'McCarthyism', as advocated by US Republican politician Joseph McCarthy (1908–1957). In 1950, McCarthy had claimed that the State Department and the US Army had been infiltrated by communists, thus creating a wave of hysteria, which continued until 1954, when he was discredited.

On 9 March 1955, at a fundraising event for the Actors Studio, Marilyn met Arthur Miller once again. It was Miller who suggested to Marilyn that she move to New York and commence training for the theatre, and in January 1956, she duly became a resident of that city.

In February 1956, Natasha Lytess of Columbia Pictures became Marilyn's drama coach: a role that she would fulfil for the next six years.

In those early days, said Miller, Marilyn 'had taken on an immanence in my imagination'. However, he expressed his doubt to her in a 'formal note saying that I wasn't the man who could make her life happen as I knew she imagined it might, and that I wished her well'.[4] Nonetheless, he subsequently confessed that 'the thought of putting Marilyn out of [his] life was unbearable'.[5]

Miller described how, during filming of *Bus Stop*, which commenced in late February 1956 and ended on 29 May, Marilyn's coach Paula Strasberg played the role of her husband Lee's 'proxy', with daily phone calls to him in New York on Marilyn's problems'.[6] Miller described Marilyn's dependence on Lee Strasberg as 'profound. If this crutch was kicked out now, she might fall'.[7]

Furthermore, Miller realised that beneath Marilyn's façade, 'all this was overlay, a swollen sea of grief heaved under it'. And he quoted Marilyn as saying:

> I don't want this, I want to live quietly, I hate it, I don't want it anymore, I want to live quietly in the country and just be there when you need me. I can't fight for myself any more.[8]

Said Miller: 'I kept trying to reassure her, but she seemed to be sinking where I could not reach. I loved her as though I had loved her all my life, her pain was mine'.[9]

On 14 May 1956, a head-and-shoulders profile of Marilyn appeared on the front cover of *Time* magazine. In an article entitled 'To Aristophanes & Back', she is described as 'the poor little waif' who had 'become a big business'.

> When Norma Jeane was twelve days old, she was put to board with a family of religious zealots who lived in a sort of 'semirural semi-slum' on the outskirts of Los Angeles. She was a normal baby, bright and happy, but when she was about two years old, she suffered a severe shock, which she insists she can remember. A

demented neighbour made a deliberate attempt to smother her with a pillow, and almost succeeded before she was dragged away.

Among her memories of this period is the recollection that at the age of six, she was raped by a grown man—'a friend', she recalls 'of the family'.

Her feelings of guilt began to be obsessive. She began to hear a noise in her head at night, and she began to brood about killing herself.

As one of the older children at the orphanage to which she was sent, the article continued:

> Norma Jeane was assigned to wash the dishes: 100 plates, 100 cups, 100 knives, forks, spoons. 'I did it three times a day, seven days a weeks', says Marilyn. 'But it wasn't so bad. It was worse to scrub out the toilets'. As payment for their work, most of the children got 5c [cents] a month. Since everybody had to put a penny in the [church collection] plate on Sunday, that left each child with 1c a month to spend. With her penny, Norma Jeane usually bought a ribbon for her hair.[10]

The research for the above article in which exaggeration, sensationalism, and downright falsehood appear to be the order of the day, was performed by Hollywood columnist and film critic Ezra Goodman.[11] However, in fairness to Goodman, he later complained that *Time*'s editors had adulterated what he had sent them. Said he:

> … the editors commended 'the absolutely first-rate' research, and then, as usual, proceeded to ignore it. What appeared in *Time* can be read in the May 14, 1956, issue of the magazine. It bears little or no relationship to the laboriously assembled and documented material that was sent to New York.[12]

In his book, *The Fifty Year Decline and Fall of Hollywood* (published in 1962), Ezra Goodman stated that he met Marilyn on a number of occasions and interviewed her, at length, during the filming of *Bus Stop* (spring 1956). He also interviewed, among others, Ida Bolender, James Dougherty, Emmeline Snively, Andre de Dienes, Paula Strasberg, Natasha Lytess, Billy Wilder, and Robert Mitchum. This, and the fact that Goodman complained bitterly about the way *Time* had adulterated his article, indicates that he is a reliable source where the life of Marilyn is concerned.

On 11 June 1956, Miller's divorce from his wife, Mary, was granted. On 21 June, he appeared before the House Un-American Activities Committee (HUAC) in Washington DC, accused of pro-communist sympathies (Miller claimed, in fact, that he had never knowingly joined the Communist Party, although he had attended its meetings). The US government was particularly annoyed with

Miller because of his 1953 play, *The Crucible*, and its implicit criticism of Joseph McCarthy.

Marilyn accompanied Miller, in order 'to give moral support during the last days of the hearing'.[13] When interviewed by the press, instead of showing anger at the way her husband had been treated, she was the epitome of dignity and charm. 'I would like to say that I'm fully confident that, in the end, my husband will win his case,' she said, smiling demurely. When she returned to New York, she and Miller 'hoped to go back to [their] normal life'.[14]

Immediately after giving testimony to the HUAC, Miller announced his intention to marry Marilyn, much to her surprise. They were married on 29 June 1956 at Westchester County Court in White Plains, New York, in a civil ceremony. It was Lee Strasberg who gave the bride away. Two days later, on 1 July, the couple participated in a traditional Jewish wedding ceremony: Marilyn having been received into the Jewish faith on that same day. Miller's family were of Polish-Jewish descent, as already mentioned. Said Susan Strasberg, daughter of Lee and Paula Strasberg: 'Marilyn insisted on converting to Judaism, although Arthur wasn't that religious. She had also wanted to please Arthur's family, now hers'.[15]

Prior to leaving with Marilyn for London on 13 July 1956 for the filming of *The Prince and the Showgirl*, in which she was to co-star with Laurence Olivier, Miller put his house at Roxbury, Connecticut, up for sale.

A few weeks later, Marilyn's confidence in her husband was shattered when she discovered an entry in his journal 'critical of her habits', and what he had written fed into all of her insecurities. Said she to Berniece:

> 'Things were never the same after I saw Arthur's note about me. I saw these horrible things he had written. I just couldn't believe it!'
>   'What do you mean, "horrible"?'
>   'Do you think being called a "bitch" is horrible?'
>   'Arthur called you a bitch?'
>   'Well, he said he agreed with Larry [Laurence Olivier] that I could be a bitch.'[16]

On 29 October 1956, Marilyn was introduced to HM Queen Elizabeth II. In late November 1956, following the completion of the filming of *The Prince and the Showgirl*, the couple returned to New York.

On 3 January 1957, the couple embarked on a fortnight's holiday in Jamaica. They subsequently took up residence at 444 East 57th Street, New York City.[17] When he and Marilyn moved into this 'spacious apartment right off the East River', said Miller:

> ... the street out front would be full of kids who cheered her when she came out of the little house. She took much pleasure in these ordinary folk and especially loved my aging father, who simply lit up at the sight of her.[18]

On 31 May 1957, Miller was found guilty of contempt, for refusing to divulge to the HUAC the names of his communist acquaintances.

In that spring of 1957, Marilyn dissolved her partnership with Milton Greene and purchased his stake in the company. For the summer, the couple rented a house at Amagansett, Long Island, New York.

In October 1957, the couple purchased a 300-acre farm at Roxbury, Connecticut, as their country retreat: 'Marilyn supervises its decoration … lovingly designing a study for Arthur. [Meanwhile] Arthur works on a screenplay that will feature Marilyn, a creation that becomes *The Misfits*.'[19]

Miller realised that his wife, Marilyn, was a very special person. Said he: 'She was a whirling light to me then, all paradox and enticing mystery, street-tough one moment, then lifted by a lyrical and poetic sensitivity that few retain past early adolescence.'[20]

Yet Marilyn's behaviour puzzled him. After one of many silences, he said to her, 'You're the saddest girl I've ever met', whereupon she smiled and replied, 'You're the only one who ever said that to me'. It was as if Miller had discerned her secret.[21]

As for Marilyn's mother, Gladys, Miller regarded her influence on her daughter as 'malign'. Gladys, he said, was a woman who 'had always been paranoid, an institutionalized schizophrenic who had tried to smother her in her crib as an infant'.[22]

However, according to the article in *Time* magazine, it was a 'demented neighbor', who had attempted to smother Marilyn. So where does the truth lie? George Barris had complained that *Time* had deliberately 'doctored' the article that he sent them on Marilyn. Furthermore, for all Miller's antipathy towards Gladys, it is likely that he was simply repeating what Marilyn had told him. Gladys's mental condition will be discussed shortly.

Prior to being interviewed by journalists, it was Marilyn's custom to insist on seeing the questions beforehand. Whereupon, she would draft the answers to these questions in her notebook. For example, in respect of her marriage to Arthur Miller she wrote: 'There was a pupil teacher relationship at the beginning of the marriage and… I learned a great deal from it'.[23]

When Marilyn was interviewed, she always appeared to look genuinely happy, regardless of the interviewer and the subject matter being discussed. However, as time went by, said Miller, 'guilt emerged as the principle of life from which neither of us could escape. Each failed with his magic to transform the other's life, and we were as we had been before, but worse; it was as though we had misled one another'.[24]

On 8 July 1958, Miller's conviction for contempt of the HUAC was overturned. Said photographer Curtice Taylor:

> … many people think that one of the reasons why they went easy on Arthur was that Marilyn showed up at those [previous] hearings and dazzled those Senators and they just left him alone.[25]

In August 1958, the couple flew to Hollywood for the filming of *Some Like It Hot,* which commenced on the 4th. Marilyn, said Berniece, had now 'grown significantly in her ability to draw emotion from audiences through the realism of her performances'.[26]

Tony Curtis, however, made the following insightful comments about the film star. She was 'in a lot of trouble. Those were difficult years for Marilyn, starting in 1956. Her personal life overwhelmed her career. There were more shots of her coming in and out of hospitals, court rooms, crying, that's what made Marilyn so vulnerable and people loved her for that because she allowed them to see that'.[27]

During the filming, continued Curtis, 'she would do a shot, and she wouldn't look at you, she'd look at Paula [Strasberg] and say, "How was that for you, Paula?"'[28]

On 16 December 1958, Marilyn suffered a miscarriage in early pregnancy.[29] Yet even as she lay on a hospital stretcher, she still managed to put on a brave face and a charming smile for the cameras.

On 19 January 1959, Marilyn received a letter from Joseph Wolhandler, vice-president of public-relations firm Rogers & Cowan, Inc., to say that the 'issue of *Life* magazine that carried [her] picture' resulted in an all-time sales record of 6,300,000 copies.[30]

*Some Like It Hot* was released on 19 March 1959 to 'immense acclaim.'[31] Subsequently, there were rumours that Marilyn was having an affair. However, said Berniece, the rumours 'were based on a series of publicity stunts to boost interest in the movie'.[32]

Miller was becoming increasingly aware that all was not well with Marilyn, but that he was powerless to do anything about it. She described herself, satirically, as 'the happy girl that all men loved', he said, but he himself 'had discovered someone diametrically opposite, a troubled woman whose desperation was deepening, no matter where she turned for a way out'.[33]

'By the start of *The Misfits*,' filming of which commenced on 21 July 1960, said Miller 'it was no longer possible to deny to [himself] that if there was a key to Marilyn's despair [he] did not possess it.[34] Throughout the filming, Paula Strasberg stuck close to Marilyn. In fact, said Miller, her control over his wife 'was now so complete that Marilyn had moved from our apartment in the hotel into hers [i.e. Paula's]'.[35]

Angela Allen, script supervisor for *The Misfits*, described how Paula was invariably attired in what was 'a black tent, really, and she had very little contact with any of the crew or Huston or Arthur Miller'.[36]

Said Eli Wallach, when a scene was shot featuring Marilyn, if Paula Strasberg did not like it, Marilyn would say, 'Could I do this scene again?' However, if Paula gave it her approval, Marilyn would say, 'Oh, I love this scene. I enjoyed this scene very much!'[37]

On one occasion, Angela Allen had a glimpse of Paula Strasberg's notebook. Said she: 'I managed to see, notated "you are a bird on a tree." It appears that is the sort of stuff she used to fill her [Marilyn] with'.[38]

Photographer Curtice Taylor was present when he overheard Paula say to Marilyn, as the scene was about to start: 'Now, Marilyn, when you're in the scene you should think onions. Think about onions'. This is the kind of stuff that she was telling her.[39] Taylor was scathing about 'The Method'— i.e. the method of teaching employed by the Strasbergs at the Actors Studio.

> Marilyn was a natural. She was a natural actress and a natural comedienne. However, as soon as she took up with Actors Studio, she became a self-conscious actor, and they were trying to put The Method on top of her. Well, The Method— you were supposed to draw on your life. Well, her life was a misery.[40]

This has a parallel with psychoanalysis that, by all accounts, Marilyn found equally painful and distasteful. So why did she stick at it? Presumably, because she thought that this was the only way for her to achieve success as an actress.

During the shooting of *The Misfits*, director John Huston said:

> [Marilyn] took so many sleeping pills to rest, that in the morning she had to take stimulants to wake her up, and this ravaged the girl. She broke down and I had to send her to a hospital for a week before we could go on with the shooting.[41]

Angela confirmed that Marilyn was developing signs of instability: 'We'd had two "rush me to the pump" [events] at night… [when] she'd overdosed and had to go and have the stomach pumped out'.[42]

After the filming, Marilyn and Miller went their separate ways. She returned to their apartment, 444 East 57th Street; he took up residence at the Adams Hotel on East 86th Street. On 11 November 1960 it was reported in the press that Marilyn and Miller's marriage was over.

On the evening of Christmas Day 1960, Marilyn received 'a forest-full of Poinsettias' with a card signed 'Best, Joe'. The flowers were from DiMaggio, who once told Marilyn that she had saved his life by sending him to a psychotherapist. She telephoned him to enquire as to why he had sent the flowers, and was told: '… first of all because I thought you would call me to thank me and then he said, besides who in the hell else do you have in the world?'.

He now asked if he might come and see Marilyn, and she agreed.[43] Perhaps DiMaggio had hopes that his romance with Marilyn might be rekindled.

On 20 January 1961, Marilyn's divorce from Miller was finalised. Following the divorce, Marilyn 'signed over to Arthur' the farmhouse that she and he had purchased and 'remodelled' in Connecticut: 'It seemed right that he should have it. I didn't want anything'.[44]

Films in which Marilyn featured between 1956 and 1960 are as follows:

## Bus Stop

Fox, August 1956
Starring Marilyn Monroe, Don Murray, Arthur O'Connell, Betty Field, and
Eileen Heckart.

In this romantic comedy, cowboy Beauregard 'Beau' (Murray) and his father-
figure friend, Virgil (O'Connell), travel from Montana to Phoenix, Arizona,
where the former is to take part in a rodeo.

At the Blue Dragon Café in Phoenix, Beau becomes infatuated with the café's
singer Chérie (Marilyn). Having bullied and attempted to kidnap Chérie, Beau,
who admits to being inexperienced with women, apologises to her.

Chérie is on her way to Hollywood, she says, 'where you get discovered'.
When she was a girl, she came second in a fashion contest: 'That's where I got my
direction. If you don't have a direction you go round and round in circles'.

In the film, Marilyn sings 'That Old Black Magic' by Harold Arlen and
Johnny Mercer. According to Berniece, Arthur was 'deeply moved by Marilyn's
performance as Chérie in *Bus Stop*'. Furthermore, critical reviews were
'uniformly excellent'.[45]

## The Prince and the Showgirl

Marilyn Monroe Productions, June 1957
Starring Marilyn Monroe and Laurence Olivier.

This romantic comedy, based on a 1953 stage play, *The Sleeping Prince*, by English
playwright Terence Rattigan, was produced and directed by English actor,
producer, and director Laurence Olivier, who also co-starred in the film. Said
Marilyn: 'I think Larry [Sir Laurence] at his best is a great actor.... But frankly,
he wasn't my choice as a director—but he wanted to direct'.[46]

The scene is set in London in 1911, prior to the coronation of George V. Among
the guests at the event are sixteen-year-old King Nicholas of Carpathia (Jeremy
Spenser), and his father Charles, the Prince Regent (Olivier).

Having watched a musical, Charles invites Elsie (Marilyn), a member of the
cast, to the embassy, intending to seduce her. She resists. She now discovers that
Nicholas is plotting against his father. Finally, she engineers a reconciliation
between father and son. In the film, Elsie is forever keeping people waiting—as
with the real-life Marilyn.

Marilyn 'idealized' her co-star Laurence Olivier, said Arthur Miller.[47]
However, she 'wanted to be a wife and at peace once this film was over with. The
filming was a kind of siege'.[48]

As for Olivier, during the filming, he admitted to Sybil Thorndike (who played
the part of the Dowager Queen) that in respect of Marilyn 'it had taken [him] quite
a few years to grasp: that for certain rare people, whose gifts were almost invisible

to the naked eye, a miracle took place in the tiny space between the lens and the negative. After working a very short time with Marilyn Monroe, [he] learnt to trust this miracle and stop gnawing [his] fingers by the side of the camera'.[49]

The outcome was, he said, that he 'was going to fall most shatteringly in love with Marilyn.... There was no question about it, it was inescapable, or so I thought; she was so adorable, so witty, such incredible fun and more physically attractive than anyone I could have imagined, apart from herself on the screen'.[50]

However, he found Marilyn's unpunctuality exasperating. On the eve of a press conference, he pleaded with her:

> Marilyn dear, please, pretty please, we cannot be late tomorrow, we cannot, they will take it very unkindly and half of them will be expecting it, so do me a favour and disappoint them, please.

In the event, 'she promised, and was [only!] one whole hour late'.[51]

Olivier remarked upon 'the technique supporting her dazzling spontaneity'.[52] He was of the opinion that it was Marilyn's training as a model, which stood her in such good stead.

> It taught her more about acting than did Lee Strasberg; my opinion of his school is that it did more harm than good to his students and that his influence on the American theatre was harmfully misapplied.[53]
>
> Marilyn was not used to rehearsing and obviously had no taste for it. She proclaimed this by her appearance—hair pulled back under a scarf, bad skin with no make-up, very dark glasses, and an overly subdued manner, which I failed dismally to find the means to enliven.[54]

However, said Berniece, from what Marilyn told her, Olivier 'spoke to her as if she was simpleminded and made light of her questions about her character's motivation'.[55]

Although Paula Strasberg was co-operative, said Olivier 'the truth came to light with uncanny speed: Paula knew nothing, she was no actress, no director, no teacher, no advisor—except in Marilyn's eyes, for she had one talent: she could butter Marilyn up'.

Olivier described a car journey, during which time Paula had acted in this way for 'a good hour, with Marilyn swallowing every word. "You are the greatest sex symbol in human memory.... You are the greatest woman of your time; of any time."' Marilyn was even more popular than Jesus Christ, in Paula's opinion.[56]

As time passed, said Olivier, Marilyn's 'manner to me got steadily ruder and more insolent'.[57]

Twenty-five years after the making of *The Prince and the Showgirl*, Olivier declared: '[After watching the film again at the behest of] a couple of my

Hollywood friends. I was as good as could be, and Marilyn! Marilyn was quite wonderful, the best of all'.[58]

As for Arthur Miller, according to Berniece, he regarded the film, which was released on 13 June 1957, as 'a trivial entertainment and her character without substance'.[59]

Although *The Prince And The Showgirl* was billed as a romantic comedy, it was overshadowed by the brooding presence of Olivier, upon whom Marilyn's behaviour had clearly taken its toll. Furthermore, his wooden and stilted performance highlighted the difference between a theatre actor and a film star in a film that is only made bearable by Marilyn's gaiety, sense of humour, and professionalism.

## Some Like It Hot
Mirish Company, March 1959
Starring Marilyn Monroe, Tony Curtis, Jack Lemmon, George Raft, Joe E. Brown, and Pat O'Brien.

Two musicians, Joe (Curtis) and Jerry (Lemmon), witness a murder by the Mafia. Following this, they dress in drag and join an all-female band in order to escape from Mafia gangsters. However, they both fall in love with Sugar (Marilyn), the band's singer and ukulele player. At one point, Sugar, who carries hip flask, says that she can stop drinking any time she wants to, but she does not want to 'especially when [she's] blue'. Again, this resonates with the real-life Marilyn.

Marilyn gives an animated performance as she enters into the spirit of this witty and romantic comedy. She sings 'Running Wild', and 'I Wanna Be Loved by You', delightfully. Yet when she sings 'I'm Thru With Love', she looks genuinely sad:

> I'm through with love
> I'll never fall again
> Said adieu to love
> Don't ever call again…

The words have a poignancy when one considers that her own emotional life was so often in turmoil.

The film was billed as 'The Most/Biggest/Hottest comedy ever made'. Said director and producer Billy Wilder of Marilyn:

> She has become a better actress, a deeper actress since Strasberg but I'm still not convinced she needed training. God gave her everything. The first day a photographer put her in front of a camera, she was a genius.[60]

*Some Like It Hot* received six Academy Award nominations, and Marilyn herself won a Golden Globe Award for best actress in a motion picture.

## Let's Make Love
Fox, September 1960
Starring Marilyn Monroe, Yves Montand, Tony Randall, and Frankie Vaughan.

It was originally intended that Marilyn should co-star with Gregory Peck. However, when Peck withdrew, his place was taken by Italian-French actor and singer Yves Montand.

Jean-Marc (Montand), a billionaire, learns that he is to be satirised in a play and he is determined to halt the production. Coffman (Tony Randall), his public relations employee, therefore suggests to him that he attends a rehearsal of the play incognito, under the pseudonym 'Alexandre Dumas'. Whereupon, singer and dancer Amanda (Marilyn) makes an entrance, sliding down a pole, dancing provocatively, and saying 'My name is Lolita and I'm not suppose to play with boys'.

When Amanda sings 'My Heart Belongs to Daddy', vivaciously and with all the appropriate expressions and mannerisms, Jean-Marc is captivated.

> While tearing off a game of golf
> I may make a play for the caddie
> But when I do, I don't follow through
> 'Cause my heart belongs to daddy

This is another irony, considering that Marilyn's own father played little or no part in her life, to her eternal regret.

In the film, the show's director does not realise that 'Alexandre Dumas' is the real-life Jean-Marc, and thinks he is merely a lookalike. The outcome is that Jean-Marc, having auditioned for the part, finds himself playing himself in the production. His motive now, however, is to insinuate himself into the life of Amanda.

Amanda remonstrates with Coffman, who has taken to the bottle, telling him, 'You don't need this stuff any more, just because you had a tough break'—which is again ironic, given Marilyn's own problems with excessive alcohol consumption.

When Jean-Marc reveals his true identity, Amanda disbelieves him and tells him that he now 'has to try to get out of the character!' Finally, the penny drops.

During the filming, Marilyn and Montand 'lived in adjacent bungalows at the Beverly Hills Hotel, and Marilyn and Yves became lovers both on and off the screen. Yves considered her just another of his conquests, but Marilyn was serious about him; she wanted him to leave his wife, [French cinema actress Simone Signoret] and she was willing to leave Arthur [Miller]'.[61]

'Simone and Arthur seemed to accept their spouses' romance as just one of those things,' said Barris.[62] Eli Wallach, however, stated that when Miller found out about Marilyn's affair with Yves Montand, he was 'very upset. It didn't make good music'.[63] Once the filming was over, continued Barris, Montand 'rushed back to France and Simone. But Marilyn never got over him'.[64]

Finally, Goodman remarked upon how, having complained to Fox about being endlessly assigned the role of a 'dumb blonde', Marilyn had subsequently been given similar dumb-blonde roles in *Bus Stop* (1956), *The Prince and the Showgirl* (1957), *Some Like It Hot* (1959), and *Let's Make Love* (1960).[66]

As for Marilyn, she considered that Amanda, in *Let's Make Love,* was the worst character that she had ever played: 'I had nothing to say. The part of the girl was awful. There was nothing there, I mean script-wise'.[66]

# Further Success for Marilyn

On 1 February 1961, *The Misfits* was released. In respect of the film, Marilyn was disappointed:

> [The director John Huston] sort of fancied himself as a writer … [and] changed it from the original intention of Arthur Miller. I personally preferred the script to be left as the writer did it. Mr. Miller at his best is a great writer.[1]

Susan Strasberg declared that subsequently, Marilyn 'hated not only the film, but herself in it. She felt it represented Arthur's real feelings for her and the whole sad end of their story'.[2]

On 29 June 1961, Marilyn underwent a cholecystectomy.[3] Said Miller: 'She seemed to see the disease as a visitation and not a consequence of immense dosages of barbiturates'.[4]

Is there a connection between inflammation of the gallbladder and excessive barbiturate ingestion? The answer is, possibly yes: the evidence being that between January 2004 and October 2012, two individuals who were taking barbiturates reported to the US Food & Drug Administration that they were suffering from chronic cholecystitis (inflammation of the gall bladder), presumably as a result.

Prior to Marilyn's operation, she told her half-sister Berniece: 'After I have surgery, I'll need somebody to be with me, especially at night. It will give us a chance to talk. I need to talk to you Berniece, and not over the telephone'.

When Berniece duly arrived, Marilyn said: 'Its so great to have you here in New York, Berniece. I'm almost glad I had surgery'. As for Berniece, she remarked: 'Remnants of [Marilyn's] childhood loneliness are swept away by the keen excitement of the reunion'.[5]

During Marilyn's convalescence, Berniece realised that Marilyn had a great deal 'on her mind.'

[Matters] seemed to weigh her down. I kept listening, trying to figure out what she wanted to say, and trying to figure out how I could help. I kept waiting for her to get around to exactly what was troubling her.[6]

She noticed, however, that Marilyn did benefit from massage, administered by 'a professional French masseur. She finds massage to be a fine therapy for sagging spirits'.[7] Also, Marilyn cherished her piano and Berniece noticed that she had painted it white.[8]

Although Joe DiMaggio's marriage to Marilyn had lasted for only nine months, the pair kept in close touch, and when he visited her during her convalescence, Berniece found him to be 'unpretentious and easy to talk to, full of common sense and concern'.[9] In fact, he 'acted as if he were still in love with Marilyn'.[10] When she suggested visiting a nightclub and restaurant, said Berniece, DiMaggio 'shakes his head determinedly. You'd be mobbed! Absolutely not'.[11]

Following her recovery from the operation, Marilyn declared: 'I just want a place I can call home'. Said Berniece, both she and DiMaggio began 'to see this desire as Marilyn's yearning for stability'.[12]

In July 1961, said Berniece, Gladys, having been confined for eight years in Rockhaven Sanitarium (i.e. since 9 February 1953), was 'officially diagnosed as a paranoid schizophrenic, one who suffers delusions of persecution'.[13]

In late July 1961, Marilyn visited Miller, bringing with her all the way from New York 'a load of belongings' to him at Roxbury Farm, Roxbury, Connecticut, by trailer.[14] Miller asked 'question after question' about Marilyn's health, said Berniece, who accompanied her half-sister. 'He's happy that she is well enough to be up and about, and says he wants her to feel truly well'. But was she sleeping any better, was she taking pills, he enquired?[15]

It was in July–August 1961, said Berniece, that Marilyn told her that she had finally met with her father:

The first time I saw my father, I was lying flat on my back in the hospital [presumably after her gallbladder surgery]. I looked at him and I studied his face and features, and I saw that Mother had told me the truth, that he was my father. I said, 'My ears are just like yours'. We talked … a long time. I enjoyed talking … with him.

Said Berniece:

I don't know how he came to be there [at the hospital] … whether he came on his own initiative, or whether she had asked him to come. She gave me the impression that he was friendly but not particularly loving or affectionate toward her. It was a mutually pleasant meeting, and they spent the time talking about the past.

Finally, Marilyn made Berniece promise that she would not divulge the identity of her father.[16] Marilyn subsequently told George Barris that even when she became successful as a movie star, her father, Charles Stanley Gifford, still refused to acknowledge her: 'He wouldn't give me the satisfaction of knowing him. He didn't want the world to know I was his love child, his mistake'.[17]

On 8 February 1962, Marilyn realised 'her dream of owning a home' when she purchased 12305, Fifth Helena Drive, Brentwood, Western LA. 'The source of her livelihood lies chiefly in Hollywood,' said Berniece, but she would retain her apartment in New York. 'Her heart is there' with DiMaggio; the Strasbergs; Miller's children, Jane and Bobby; and his father, Isidore Miller; poet and novelist Norman Rosten, his wife, Hedda, and their daughter, Patricia; 'and with other good friends'.[18] Marilyn flew all the way to Mexico to find decorations for the house.[19] Even though the property was being remodelled and as yet lacked furniture, it gave her 'a tremendous feeling of pride. She was so excited that she invited everyone to see it in spite of the mess. Joe DiMaggio was pleased to see her happy involvement and admired each change she made. He was on the telephone with her nearly every day and visited whenever he was in California'.[20]

However, Marilyn told Barris that for her, life at Brentwood was not all a bed of roses.

> I live here all alone with my snowball, my little white poodle—he was given to me by my dear old friend Frank Sinatra. I call him Maf. Oh sure, it gets lonesome at times living alone; I'd rather be married and have children and a man to love—but you can't always have everything in life the way you want it. You have to accept what comes your way. I live alone and I hate it.[21]

## The Misfits
Seven Arts Productions, 1961
Starring Clark Gable, Marilyn Monroe, and Montgomery Clift.

This film drama is based on an eponymous novella, written by Arthur Miller in 1957. He also wrote the screenplay.

Recently divorced Roslyn (Marilyn) meets ageing cowboy Gaylord (Gable) and his friend, Guido (Eli Wallach), in a bar. Whereupon, Roslyn and her friend, Isabelle (Thelma Ritter), are invited to stay with the men at Guido's country home in Nevada. Gaylord is also a divorcee, and Guido is a widower. Seeking a third hand to help them round up some wild mustangs, they attend a rodeo and engage Perce (Clift) for the task.

Roslyn falls in love with Gaylord, only to discover that the mustangs are to be sold for dog food. She now regards the cowboy as a killer, and eventually, she persuades him to release the mustangs.

Miller's *The Misfits* contained many parallels to his and Marilyn's own lives. For example, Roslyn (Marilyn) was a wounded and vulnerable young woman who falls in love with Gaylord (Gable), an older man.

The film also reflects Marilyn's love of animals and her abhorrence of animal cruelty. For example, when a mustang has to be put down, she becomes extremely agitated, and screams at the cowboys, 'Killers! Murderers!'

Filming of *The Misfits* commenced on 21 July 1960, during the course of which Marilyn told her co-star, US film actor Clark Gable 'that he had been her girlhood idol; in fact, his framed photo stood on her equally worshipful mother's bureau, and in her very earliest years Marilyn thought he was her father.'[22]

It was on the set of *The Misfits* that Miller met Inge Morath, who would become his third and last wife. An Austrian-born US photographer working for Magnum Photos Agency, she had been sent to cover the filming, which ended on 4 November 1960.

Twelve days later, on 16 November 1960, Clark Gable died of a heart attack.

On 17 February 1962, Arthur Miller married Inge Morath.

## 12

# Myths and Rumours

*Most of the highly publicized Marilyn Monroe legend about her family background and upbringing has been revealed as being nothing more than a legend. There are grounds for being skeptical about a good many other aspects of the Monroe story.*[1]

Ezra Goodman

George Barris stated that Marilyn had been reticent about certain aspects of her life for fear of adverse publicity. Said he:

I realized why she had kept secret for so long that her mother was alive but in a mental hospital, and why she told no one about the nude calendar picture for which she posed when she was young and broke. Neither was a matter of shame for her, but she was afraid that revealing the truth might damage or even end her fabulous career.[2]

However, evidence points to the fact that Marilyn did more than simply keep silent. In spring 1948, Grace Goddard spoke to Berniece on the telephone in respect of 'the story that she and Marilyn have just invented'. Said she:

We had to have a biographical story and we had to have one fast! We hadn't dreamed that we would need one, and suddenly things were happening too fast. We made up a story about Marilyn having no parents and being in a lot of foster homes and spending time in an orphanage and Marilyn signed it as being the truth.

Berniece said:

Their breathless fantasy seems unrestrained by the fact that Gladys is often at Marilyn's side. They know that the public loves a rags-to-riches drama.

That story was Grace's idea. She built it around the fact that Marilyn had spent time in an orphanage. Other than that, it wasn't true, but the story served its publicity purpose. And it kept reporters away from Mameta [Berniece's nickname for her mother Gladys].[3]

In other words, according to Berniece, both Marilyn and Grace were complicit in creating part of the 'legend' that Goodman referred to.

According to Marilyn's former foster mother, Ida Bolender, other accounts of Marilyn's life were equally false. Writing from Hawthorne, California, to Berniece Miracle on 8 August 1962, Ida said, in respect of Marilyn: 'It has almost broken my heart to read the terrible stories that have been written about her early childhood, when I know personally they are so untrue'.[4]

Harry Brand, head of the publicity department at Fox, told Goodman:

[With US actress Shirley Temple] we had twenty rumors a year that she was kidnapped. With [Betty] Grable, we had twenty rumors a year that she was raped. With Monroe, we have twenty rumors a year that she has been raped and kidnapped.[5]

Marilyn was approaching the age of thirty when, as already mentioned, on 14 May 1956, an article appeared in *Time* magazine. It stated that, among Marilyn's memories, a 'demented neighbour' had attempted to smother her when she was 'about two years old', and that when she was aged six, a grown man—'a friend of the family'—had raped her. Marilyn must surely have been aware of this article, but she evidently made no attempt to contradict it.

As regards the alleged attempted smothering of Marilyn, while it cannot be definitively ruled out, the memories of a two-year-old should be treated with caution. As for the alleged rape, Marilyn's first husband, James Dougherty, affirmed that his bride was a virgin when he married her, so this was simply untrue. However, it does not preclude the possibility that Marilyn was sexually abused at this time.

Elizabeth Loftus, Professor of Law and Cognitive Science at the University of California, Irvine, declared as follows, in respect of false memories from childhood: 'We pick up information from all sorts of places and times and use it to "create" our memories'.[6]

# Marilyn in Profile

### Marilyn as a Child
Marilyn stated that, as a teenager, she was 'an intense introvert probably'.[1]

### Marilyn the Homemaker
As a homemaker, Marilyn was thorough and meticulous and made detailed lists of furnishings, foodstuffs, and recipes—cooking clearly being a hobby of hers.[2] James Dougherty, her first husband, attested to the fact that her cooking was 'fairly good, especially if she followed a cookbook carefully'.[3]

### Relaxation: Sociability
Ezra Goodman stated:

> [Although Marilyn] takes hours to get her hairdo and make-up just right for public appearances… privately, she likes to scamper about without any make-up at all and with her hair dishevelled.[4]

In regard to socialising, Marilyn told George Barris: 'I've never been a night clubber'. She preferred to visit her friends at their homes, or to attend their house parties.[5] 'I've never been very good at being a member of any group—more than a group of two that is,' she said.[6] She confessed: '[There were] days or weeks when I wanted only to have occasional company when desired [and to] busy myself in reading'.[7] Finally, she said: 'I am at ease with people I trust or admire'.[8]

Barris said: '[Marilyn] liked more than anything to stay at home and read a book or listen to her favourite Judy Garland and Frank Sinatra recordings'.[9]

### Role Models
Marilyn described how she 'had always felt a need to live up to that expectation of my elders'.[10] She admired Greta Garbo 'for her artistic creativity and her personal courage and integrity'.[11]

'The truth can only be recalled, never invented,' said Marilyn.[12] This was a tenet that she tried to emulate, though she did not always succeed.

## Self-deprecation
'I have a strong sense of self criticism,' she declared.[13]

## Naïveté
Robert Mitchum told Goodman that, in 1953, during the filming of *River of No Return*, 'Marilyn was reading a dictionary of Freudian terms'. When she reached the chapter headed 'Anal Eroticism', she asked Mitchum, first, 'What's eroticism', and then, 'What's anal?'[14]

## Nervousness, Anxiety, and Insecurity
US actor George Chakiris observed Marilyn in spring 1953, during the filming of *Gentlemen Prefer Blondes*. He later recalled that she was 'sitting on the round sofa used during the song, and [he] noticed the muscles in her back quivering from nerves'.[15]

To her psychotherapist, Dr Margaret H. Hohenberg, Marilyn wrote in that same year, 1956: 'I keep feeling I won't be able to do the part when I have to, it's like a horrible nightmare'.[16]

In a typed note, probably written in 1943, during the second year of her marriage to Dougherty, Marilyn made several mentions of her sense of insecurity.[17]

## Vulnerability
In spring 1956, Goodman said:

> Underneath the highly-publicized sexpot is a little girl who arouses the protective instinct in many people, both female and male. This lost little girl element in her emotional make-up may well be the vital thing that has endeared her to the world. In actuality, she is more a child than siren.[18]

## Industriousness
In spring 1947, Berniece stated that Marilyn 'prefers work to socialising. She is an incipient workaholic'.[19]

In 1962, in answer to possible future questions from journalists about what her priorities were, Marilyn replied: 'the love of my work and a few reliable human beings'.[20]

In an undated note Marilyn wrote: 'I must try to work and work on my concentration'.[21] Another undated note from her address book reads:

> Must make effort to do

must have the discipline to do the following:

z: go to class—my own always—without fail

x: go as often as possible to observe Strasberg's other private classes

g: never miss my actors studio sessions

v: work whenever possible—on class assignments—and always keep working on the acting exercises.[22]

On 19 December 1961, Marilyn wrote at length to Lee Strasberg, and described what made her a driven person:

> As you know, for years I have been struggling to find some emotional security with little success, for many different reasons. Only in the last several months, as you detected, do I seem to have made a modest beginning. It is true that my treatment with Dr. [Ralph] Greenson [her psychiatrist and psychoanalyst] has had its ups and downs, as you know. However my overall progress is such that I have hopes of finally establishing a piece of ground for myself to stand on, instead of the quicksand I have always been in. But Dr. Greenson agrees with you, that for me to live decently and productively, I must work. And work means not merely performing professionally, but to study and truly devote myself. My work is the only trustworthy hope I have.[23]

### Strength of Character: Determination to Improve Herself

In spring 1956, Joseph M. Schenck of Fox told Goodman: '[Marilyn] always wanted to learn something. If she came to dinner and a good smart man was at dinner, I'd always put her alongside that man. She always wanted to improve herself'.[24]

In 1962, Marilyn wrote: 'I constantly try to clarify and redefine my goals'.[25] On a scrap of paper, Marilyn made this undated entry: 'for life: It is rather a determination not to be overwhelmed'.[26]

### The Importance of Being 'Well Turned Out'

In autumn 1946, Berniece stated:

> Norma Jeane always got up early and pressed her skirt before going to work. She said that most of the other starlets came to work in slacks or were sloppily dressed, and some of them wore dirty shoes, or didn't have their hair fixed. Norma Jeane thought it was very important to look neat from the start. Regardless of what was scheduled for her at the studio, she went there every single day as neat as a pin.[27]

Subsequent films taken of Marilyn show that although she sometimes dressed casually, she almost always looked smart.

## Shrewdness

Lucille Ryman of MGM told Goodman that 'under Marilyn's baby-doll, kitten exterior, she is tough and shrewd and calculating, or she wouldn't be where she is today'.[28]

## The Myth of Marilyn as a 'Dumb Blonde'

Berniece said:

> [Although Marilyn] left high school after the eleventh grade, and although there were gaps in her general knowledge, she had a good academic record and throughout her life was a voracious reader. Marilyn's constant reading only seemed to earn her criticism and ridicule. The real Marilyn was thought to be the phony one.[29] [Furthermore] To Marilyn, it seems that the public is both confused and angered by her refusal to conform to the dumb blonde image it holds of her.[30]

Said Barris: 'Marilyn had a great love for the arts—acting, dancing, music, poetry, and literature'. She had studied literature and art at UCLA, as already mentioned, and 'not graduating was her one big regret in life'.[31]

## Talents

As already mentioned, Marilyn was a competent pianist and a composer of poems.

In her writings, although her syntax is often somewhat disjointed, and her spelling leaves a lot to be desired, from the language that Marilyn uses, it is clear that here is a person of great talent and sensitivity. For example, the phrases 'secret mid-night meetings'; 'the fugetive [fugitive] glance stolen in others' company'; 'the sharing of the ocean, moon & stars'; and 'air aloneness', from a typed note that she made *circa* 1943.[32]

'I love poetry and poets,' she said, and yes, it is true, there was a poetic quality to many of her compositions.[33] However, she admitted that it was 'very difficult for [her] to get down on paper as if talking to a second person those bare truths & emotions [she] felt—perhaps even poetic'.[34]

## Poetry

On 2 March 1961, Marilyn told Dr Greenson that she was currently reading Irish playwright Sean O'Casey's first autobiography, and said that he had once composed a poem and sent it to her.[35]

## Painting and Sculpture

In her notebook, *circa* 1951, Marilyn made notes on the Florentine Renaissance, and on some of its principal artists, architects, and painters. In 1956, at Los Angeles, she was photographed standing beside a sculpture by Edgar Degas.[36]

In May 1962, she purchased a bronze copy of French sculptor Auguste Rodin's sculpture *The Embrace*, and an oil painting by French artist Nicola Ortis Poucette, entitled *La Toureau (The Bull)*.[37]

## Literature

In spring 1956, Natasha Lytess told Goodman that she had 'introduced her [Marilyn] to books—[Rainer Maria] Rilke's *Letters to a Young Poet* and others'.[38] Referring to the year 1962, Marilyn stated: 'At the present time I'm reading Capt. [*Captain*] *Newman M.D.* [by US humourist Leo Calvin Rosten] and *To Kill a Mockingbird* [by US novelist Harper Lee]'.[39]

Many photographs exist of Marilyn reading books; for example, by German poet and essayist Heinrich Heine.[40] In 1953, she was filmed reading a book about the artist Goya.[41] In summer 1955, she was filmed reading Irish writer James Joyce's novel *Ulysses*, albeit with a somewhat bemused look on her face—which is hardly surprising![42] In the same year, in New York, she was filmed reading *To The Actor: On the Technique of Acting* by Michael Chekhov, and US poet Walt Whitman's poetry collection *Leaves of Grass*.[43, 44]

A cynic might conclude that Marilyn was only pretending to read these books. However, it is pointed out that her personal library contained works by the authors John Steinbeck, Albert Camus, Ernest Hemingway, Gustave Flaubert, Samuel Beckett, Joseph Conrad, John Milton, Kahlil Gibran, and many others.[45]

## Her Acquaintance with Artistic and Literary Figures

On 28 October 1926, Marilyn was invited by English poet Edith L. Sitwell to meet her at the Sesame Club at 49 Grosvenor Street, London, where the two discussed the poetry of Gerald Manley Hopkins and Dylan Thomas. Edith described Marilyn as 'extremely intelligent' and 'exceedingly sensitive'.[46]

In New York, in 1959, Marilyn was photographed at the house of US novelist and poet Carson McCullers at a luncheon given in honour of the Danish writer Karen Blixen.[47]

On 31 January 1961, British writer W. Somerset Maugham wrote to Marilyn to thank her for her 'charming telegram of good wishes on [his] birthday'.[48]

## Compassion: Humaneness

'I have great feeling for all the persecuted ones in the world,' said Marilyn in 1962.[49] She wrote of Eleanor Roosevelt (1884–1962), wife of President Franklin D. Roosevelt, and 'her devotion to mankind', and of US poet Carl Sandburg (1878–1967), and how 'his poems are songs of the people by the people and for people'.[50]

Of President John F. Kennedy and his brother, Robert, she wrote: 'they symbolize the youth of America—in its vigor its brilliance and its compassion'.[51] On 2 February 1962, Marilyn wrote to Arthur Miller's son, Robert 'Bobby':

I had dinner last night with the Attorney-General of the United States, Robert Kennedy, and I asked him what his department was going to do about Civil Rights and some other issues.

'The youth of America want answers,' she said.[52]

On the same day, she wrote to Arthur Miller's father, Isidore, to tell him that what she liked best about Robert Kennedy was 'his Civil Rights program' and his 'wonderful sense of humor'.[53]

## Love of Children

Berniece described Marilyn's happy relationship with her daughter, Mona Rae, with whom she would play 'Chopsticks' on the black Franklin grand piano (manufactured by the Franklin Piano Company of New York City, founded in 1887) in Aunt Ana's living room.[54] Referring to 'her little niece Mona Rae [born 18 July 1939]', Marilyn declared: 'she's pretty and sweet and soft, and she smells good and I feel good when she hugs me'.[55]

Dougherty stated that Marilyn liked children 'and knew how to take care of them'. For example, in 1943, Dougherty's brother Marion's children (by his first wife, Yuma), visited the Dougherty family home in Van Nuys. Whereupon, 'it fell upon Norma Jean[e] to look after them. For two or three weeks, she fed them, saw that they had clean clothes, took daily baths, and she played with them. She sang to them and read them the funny papers. Just her presence in a room with them seemed to keep them content'.[56]

In July 1961, Berniece stated that Marilyn had become 'extremely fond' of Joe DiMaggio's son, Joe (junior, born 23 October 1941). When he was a teenager, said Marilyn, and 'having the usual young teenager problems.... Mostly I just listened to him. I love doing things with him, and I gave him spending money from time to time and little things'.[57]

Marilyn also confessed to missing Jane Ellen (born 7 September 1944) and Robert 'Bobby' Arthur (born 31 May 1947), Miller's children by his first wife, Mary Slattery.

During the filming of *Something's Got to Give*, in spring 1962, two little children were involved in a swimming pool scene. In order to put them at their ease, Marilyn cuddled them and romped with them on the grass—to the obvious delight of all parties.[58]

## Love of Animals

According to Berniece, Marilyn's 'lifelong love of animals begins with her mutt Tippy. She suffers terrible grief when Tippy is shot by a neighbor'.[59]

The shooting occurred in June 1933, when Marilyn was aged seven. Anything more heart-breaking for a little girl, and especially for one in Marilyn's position, can scarcely be imagined. Tippy was yet another loving companion to be taken away from her during her childhood.

In summer 1943, said Dougherty, when he and Marilyn had been married for almost a year:

> … some friends had given us a collie we named Muggsie. Muggsie was a lady with long white and brown hair, and she looked just as shiny and fresh-scrubbed all the time as her mistress. Norma Jean bathed her nearly every day. Muggsie was, in a way, a substitute for the child she wanted very badly.[60]

'One rainy day,' said Dougherty, during the period of his marriage to Marilyn, she 'saw a cow standing in the rain mooing and she wanted to bring it into the living room'.[61]

Referring to the year 1958, said Berniece, Marilyn had a dog: 'Hugo the basset hound, who travels back and forth from Roxbury to Manhattan on each trip, for Marilyn's fondness for dogs is second only to her love of children'.[62]

In May 1961, Marilyn was given a poodle called 'Maf'—Maf being short for Mafia—by US singer and film actor Frank Sinatra. The dog, said Marilyn, 'just *looks* like a piece of the rug. He didn't like getting his hair cut, so I left it full and fluffy. Now I like it that way'.[63]

### Views about Parenthood

When she was in her early thirties, Marilyn told Barris:

> The thing I want more than anything else? I want a baby! I want to have children! I used to feel [that] for every child I had, I would adopt another, but I don't think a single person should adopt children. There's no Ma or Pa there.[64]

Sadly, because of repeated miscarriages, she would never become a mother.

### Generosity

Marilyn supported several charitable causes: in particular, those relating to the young. For example, the Milk Fund for Babies and the March of Dimes for children suffering from poliomyelitis. She was lavish with her gifts to family members, and also to friends and colleagues in need.

Marilyn was also generous in her praise for fellow film stars such as Greta Garbo, Jeanne Eagels, Laurette Taylor, Jean Harlow, and Kay Kendall.[65]

### Disinterest in Materialism

Marilyn told Barris: 'I'm not interested in being a millionaire. The one thing a person wants most in life is usually something basic that money can't buy'.[66]

### Faith

In her youth, Marilyn had been brought up to be a Christian Scientist. Dougherty stated:

> She had a true love of God and Christ, even though she had stopped attending even the Christian Science church when we got married. She still believed in the Bible and in the Ten Commandments.[67]

The founder of the Christian Science Church was Mary Baker Eddy (1821–1910), born in Bow, New Hampshire, USA, whose book, *Science and Health with Key to the Scriptures* (published in 1875), proclaimed that physical disease was an illusion. Marilyn stated: 'Scientists believe in mind over matter. Mind causes disease. Mind also cures disease. They don't believe in taking medicines'.[68]

She herself, however, was more pragmatic, and declared that she was 'not too good at practicing that part of it'. Instead, she declared: 'I take … prescriptions, stuff for cramps'.[69]

Lee and Paula Strasberg's daughter, Susan, an actress, said this of Marilyn: that having been married to Arthur Miller, 'she referred to herself as "an atheist Jew", saying, "I believe in everything a little.… Anyway, I can identify with the Jews. Everybody's always out to get them, no matter what they do, like me."'

> She was so sceptical of all organised religion from her childhood contacts. Most of the religious people she had known were 'devout hypocrites', although she liked the ideas embodied in the Christian Science church.[70]

## Love, Sexuality, Faithfulness, and Heartache

Said Dougherty, Marilyn 'believed that sex was for a husband and wife; it was not for promiscuous display'.[71] However, in respect of her first husband, Marilyn stated as follows:

> The unfortunate thing was that any withdrawing or coldness was deliberate [i.e. on her part], and that although I recognized this feeling, I had no desire except in very passionate moods to overcome my feelings. Very few people, except my more sensitive acquaintances, sensed this and accepted it fully, he did not.[72]

Harry Lipton of the Helen Ainsworth Agency, with whom Marilyn signed a contract on 11 March 1946, opined to Goodman that Marilyn 'brings out the desire in people to help her, to protect her, to mother and father her. It's not a sex thing at all. She's playing a role—this sex thing'.[73]

André de Dienes told Goodman in spring 1956, during the filming of *Bus Stop*, that 'Marilyn is not sexy at all. She has very little feeling towards sex. She is not sensuous. Since she is not the slave of sex, her work comes first'.[74]

The following lines by Marilyn, composed in July 1956, the month after her marriage to Miller, when she was in England for the filming of *The Prince and the Showgirl*, beg the question, was she capable of real love?

To have your heart is
the only completely happy proud thing (that ever belonged
to me) I've ever possessed so
I guess I have always been
deeply terrified to really be someone's
wife
since I know from life
one cannot love another,
ever, really.[75]

In that same month of July 1956, Marilyn appeared to be frightened that the passage of time might diminish her, in the eyes of her husband, Arthur Miller. From the tone of her writing, it seems likely that these lines were composed following her discovery of derogatory comments made by Miller about her in his diary.

where his eyes rest with pleasure—I
want to still be—but time has changed
the hold of that glance.
Alas how will I cope when I am
even less useful—

I seek joy but it is clothed
with pain—
take heart as in my youth
sleep and rest my heavy head
on his breast for still my love
sleeps beside me.[76]

During their time in London in summer 1956, Marilyn and Miller resided at Parkside House, Englefield Green, Surrey. On their host's notepaper, headed with the above address, Marilyn made notes and wrote poetry. If the following poem refers to her marriage, it suggests that Miller is in love with somebody else and that she is, in consequence, bereft.

*my love sleeps besides me—*
*in the faint light—I see his manly jaw...*

*the pain of his longing when he looks*
*at another—*
*like an unfulfillment since the day*
*he was born.*

*And I in merciless pain*
*and with his pain of longing—*
*when he looks at and loves another*
*like an unfulfillment of the day*
*he was born—*
*we must endure*
*I more sadly because I can feel no joy.*[77]

Was Miller really in love with somebody else, and not with his wife, Marilyn? Or, as seems more likely, was this merely groundless anxiety on her part?

In spring 1958, in the second year of her marriage to Miller, Marilyn wrote as follows, 're-relationships':

> how do we know the pain of another's earlier years let alone
> all that he drags with him since along the way at best a lot of lee-way is
> needed for the other—yet how much is unhealthy for one to bear.

She concludes: 'I think to love bravely is the best and accept—as much as one can bear'.[78] In other words, relationships can, for historical reasons, be something of an ordeal. Furthermore, the following lines, written by Marilyn at about the same time, confirm that her own marriage was in deep trouble.

> Roxbury [the home that Marilyn and Miller purchased in the previous summer of 1957]—I've tried to imagine spring all winter—it's here and I still feel hopeless. I think I hate it here because there is no love here anymore.[79]

In other words, by spring 1958, Marilyn's marriage to Miller was virtually over, even though the couple did not divorce for another three years.

Said Marilyn: 'I would like to be in love. I hate living alone'.[80] This, presumably, was said after her divorce from Miller in January 1961. As regards Marilyn's three former husbands, said Barris: '…she had loved them as best as she could, but she had probably never been in love with any of them'.[81]

## Attitude to Nudity

As regards nudity, Dougherty said: '[Marilyn] loved to be nude around the house, but to be nude in front of the world must have been a nightmare to her'.[82] How ironic it is that the woman who was considered to be the world's greatest sex symbol may not actually have been in love with any of her three former spouses, and showed only limited interest in sexual intercourse.

# Marilyn's Continuing Need for an Attachment Figure

As psychologist John Bowlby said, and as has already been mentioned:

> ... the requirement of an attachment figure, a secure personal base, [is] by no means confined to children. There are good reasons for believing ... that the requirement applies also to adolescents, and to mature adults as well.[1]

The film *River of No Return* (1954), in which Marilyn featured as a singer in a saloon bar, was directed by Otto Preminger. When Preminger barred Natasha Lytess from the set, studio head Darryl Zanuck countermanded Preminger's order to keep Marilyn happy.[2] Ezra Goodman stated:

> Lytess told me that Monroe put her on a spot with directors and studios in Hollywood by insisting that she be on the set with her and guide her, acting-wise, from behind the camera. This aroused resentment on the part of many directors and did not help Lytess professionally.[3]

As for Natasha, she said in respect of Marilyn:

> I worked with her on every line, every gesture, every breath, every movement of the eyes. I worked on all her dances and songs. Marilyn wouldn't move without me. She needed me like a dead man needs a casket. I have letters in my drawer saying she needs me much more than her life.[4]

During the filming of *The Misfits* (1961), Angela Allen said that John Huston and Billy Wilder agreed that 'there was no point, at the beginning, in sort of having a stand-up row with Paula [Strasberg], because Marilyn was totally dependent upon her [i.e. as her drama coach]'.[5]

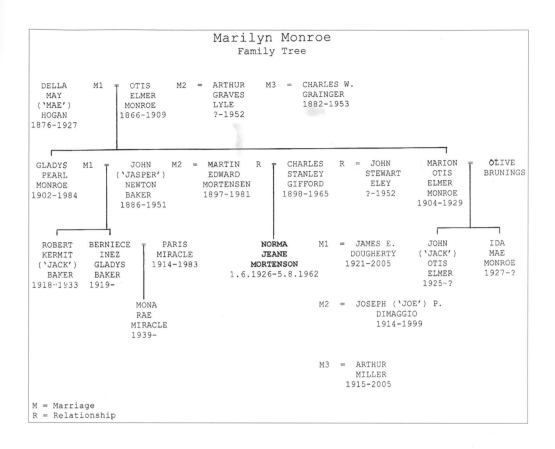

# Marilyn Monroe
## Family Tree

| | M1 | | M2 | | M3 | |
|---|---|---|---|---|---|---|
| DELLA MAY ('MAE') HOGAN 1876–1927 | | OTIS ELMER MONROE 1866–1909 | | ARTHUR GRAVES LYLE ?–1952 | | CHARLES W. GRAINGER 1882–1953 |

| GLADYS PEARL MONROE 1902–1984 | M1 | JOHN ('JASPER') NEWTON BAKER 1886–1951 | M2 | MARTIN EDWARD MORTENSEN 1897–1981 | R | CHARLES STANLEY GIFFORD 1898–1965 | R | JOHN STEWART ELEY ?–1952 | | MARION OTIS ELMER MONROE 1904–1929 | | OLIVE BRUNINGS |

| ROBERT KERMIT ('JACK') BAKER 1918–1933 | BERNIECE INEZ GLADYS BAKER 1919– | PARIS MIRACLE 1914–1983 | **NORMA JEANE MORTENSON** 1.6.1926–5.8.1962 | M1 | JAMES E. DOUGHERTY 1921–2005 | JOHN ('JACK') OTIS ELMER 1925–? | IDA MAE MONROE 1927–? |

MONA RAE MIRACLE 1939–

M2 = JOSEPH ('JOE') P. DIMAGGIO 1914–1999

M3 = ARTHUR MILLER 1915–2005

M = Marriage
R = Relationship

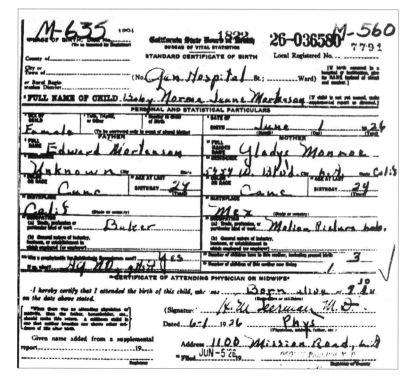

*Above:* Marilyn Monroe's family tree.

*Right:* Marilyn— baptised Norman Jeane Mortenson.

An outing to the beach, Marilyn front left, her mother, Gladys, rear left (unknown photographer).

*Left:* Marilyn, aged about ten years (unknown photographer).

*Opposite:* Marilyn as a teenager (unknown photographer).

*Above:* Boating scene, Marilyn centre (unknown photographer).

*Opposite:* Marilyn, a rising star (unknown photographer).

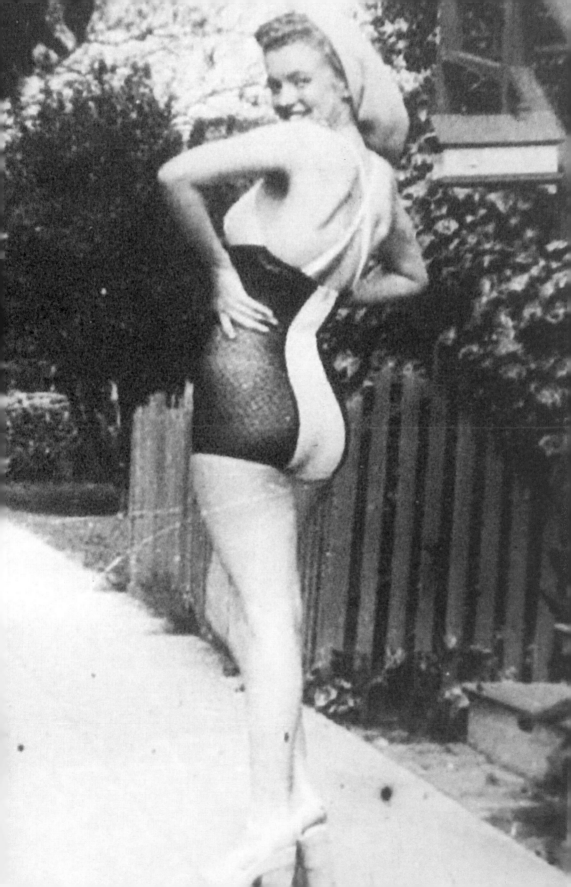

*Opposite:* Marilyn and James Dougherty on their wedding day, 19 June 1942.

*Above:* Marilyn and James Dougherty, marriage certificate.

16315 $1.95

# the secret
# happiness of
# MARILYN
# MONROE

marilyn's first husband talks about
his teenage bride, their life together, and
the ambitions that tore them apart
**by james e. dougherty**

exclusive! never before told

**BONUS**

A
COLLECTION
OF RARE
EARLY PHOTOS

James Dougherty's biography of Marilyn.

# My Sister Marilyn

## A MEMOIR OF MARILYN MONROE

**BERNIECE BAKER MIRACLE and MONA RAE MIRACLE**

Berniece Miracle (*née* Baker) and her daughter's, Mona Rae Miracle, *Memoir* of Marilyn. Berniece on left, Marilyn on right.

*Above:* Marilyn in 1950 (unknown photographer).

*Opposite above:* Marilyn and Joe DiMaggio (unknown photographer).

*Opposite below:* Marilyn and Joe DiMaggio, marriage certificate.

Marilyn Monroe, *Time* magazine, 14 May 1956.

Above left: Marilyn and Arthur Miller. (*Photo: Press Association*)

Above right: Sir Laurence Olivier and Marilyn. (*Photo: Tra Rosenberg, New York Herald Tribune, 10 February 1956*)

Below: Dame Edith Sitwell and Marilyn, Hollywood, 1953. (*Photo by George Silk, Time magazine*)

HER LIFE IN HER OWN WORDS

*Marilyn*

MARILYN
MONROE'S
REVEALING
LAST WORDS
AND
PHOTOGRAPHS

●

GEORGE BARRIS

*Above:* George Barris's biography of Marilyn.

*Opposite above:* Marilyn with George Barris in 1962, on the set of *Something's Got to Give.*
(*Photo: New York Post: Getty images*)

*Opposite below left:* Some Like It Hot.

*Opposite below right:* Something's Got to Give.

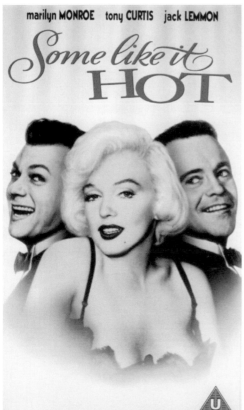

marilyn **MONROE**   tony **CURTIS**   jack **LEMMON**

# Some like it HOT

*Hawaii*

## MARILYN: SOMETHING'S GOT TO GIVE

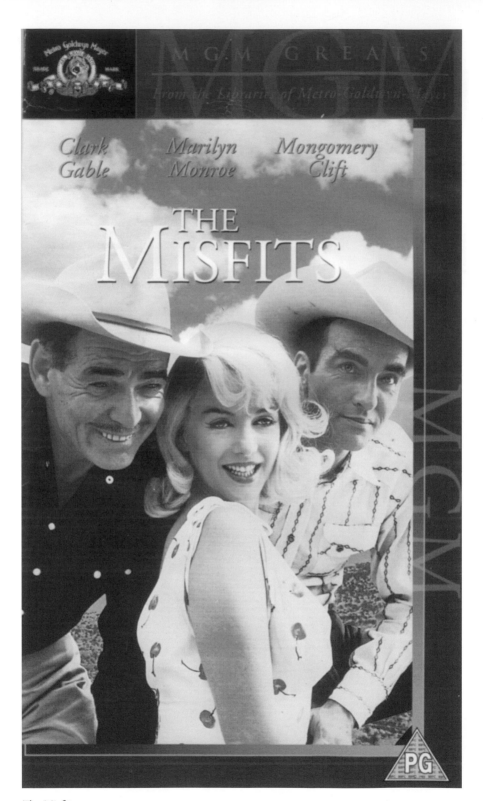

The Misfits.

Referring to a scene where Marilyn had to ascend some steps, Cyd Charisse declared: 'Marilyn went up and down those stairs ten or twelve times and every time she would go up the stairs she would look at Paula and if Paula said no then she had to do it again'.[6]

Clearly, Marilyn regarded the aforementioned 'attachment figures' as vital to her wellbeing, and to her ability to function.

# Encounters with Psychiatrists and other Would-Be Diagnosticians

In early 1951, Marilyn consulted psychiatrist Dr Judd Marmor of LA. This, said Berniece, 'was to be the beginning of a long and often painful journey into psychoanalysis, which was to last until the very end of her life'.[1]

In 1951, commencing in January, Marilyn had a love affair with film producer Elia Kazan. Said she, Kazan described her as 'the gayest girl he ever knew and believe me he has known many. But he loved me for one year and once rocked me to sleep one night when I was in great anguish. He also suggested that I go into analysis and later wanted me to work with his teacher, Lee Strasberg'.[2]

In early February 1955, prior to accepting Marilyn as a student, Lee Strasberg made it a condition of his accepting her as a drama student that she commenced psychoanalysis. Lee Strasberg encouraged psychoanalysis, said Berniece: '… almost as a part of training for his students. He felt that whatever helped actors gain insight into their feelings was good'.[3]

Marilyn, therefore, approached Hungarian-born Dr Margaret H. Hohenberg, Freudian psychoanalyst of New York City, under whom Milton Greene himself was currently undergoing psychoanalysis.[4] The outcome was that from mid-February 1955, Marilyn underwent sessions of psychoanalysis and therapy with Dr Hohenberg.

In August 1956, while in London, Marilyn commenced psychoanalysis with psychoanalyst Anna Freud, daughter of Austrian neurologist and founder of psychoanalysis, Sigmund Freud (1856–1939).[5] In March 1957, on the advice of her husband, Arthur Miller, Marilyn sought the advice of a different psychoanalyst, and Anna Freud recommended that she consult her friend, Viennese-born Dr Marianne Kris (*née* Ries) of New York City. Marilyn now commenced therapy sessions with Dr Kris—five days per week. Berniece said that Marilyn liked her new therapist 'very much'.[6]

In January 1960, Dr Kris recommended Marilyn to a colleague of hers in LA: Dr Ralph Greenson of Beverly Hills. Greenson was a founder member of the Los

Angeles Psychoanalytic Society and many of his patients were Hollywood film stars.

On 18 July 1960, Marilyn commenced regular psychotherapy sessions with Dr Greenson. He insisted that she obtained his prescribed medication from her general physician Dr Hyman Engelberg, also of Beverly Hills. In December 1960, Marilyn resumed psychotherapy with Dr Kris.[7]

In early February 1961, Marilyn's condition was giving cause for concern. She had shut herself away at home; was eating little; losing weight; and relying on sleeping tablets. On 5 February, a concerned Dr Kris drove her to the Payne Whitney Psychiatric Clinic, New York City, where she was admitted to the security wing and locked in a padded cell. Susan Strasberg said that Dr Kris 'felt Marilyn was at a point of no return and that she had to go into the hospital to detoxify from all that substance abuse'.[8]

To Lee and Paula Strasberg on 7 February 1961, Marilyn wrote:

> Dr Kris has had me put into the New York Hospital—psychiatric division under the care of two idiot doctors—they both should not be my doctors. You haven't heard from me because I'm locked up with all these poor nutty people. I'm sure to end up a nut if I stay in this nightmare.[9]

On 10 February 1961, Marilyn was released from hospital, when her former husband, Joe DiMaggio, intervened on her behalf. Following this, Dr Kris conveyed her to the Columbia Presbyterian Medical Center, New York City, for a three-week period of recuperation.[10]

On 2 March 1961, Marilyn forwarded some notes that she had made to Dr Greenson. She described how, as a patient in Payne Whitney Hospital, she had looked out of the window and seen the trees:

> [The trees] give me a little hope—the desolate bare branches promising maybe there will be spring and maybe they promise hope. Last night I was awake all night again. Sometimes I wonder what the night time is for. It almost doesn't exist for me—it all seems like one long, long horrible day. Anyway, I thought I'd try to be constructive about it and started to read the letters of Sigmund Freud. When I first opened the book I saw the picture of Freud inside opposite the title page and I burst into tears—he looked very depressed. I see a sad disappointment in his gentle face.

Having a mother who had mental health problems and spent many years in psychiatric hospitals, the effect of this forced, nightmarish incarceration must have led Marilyn to question her own sanity. She continued:

> There was no empathy at Payne-Whitney—it had a very bad effect—they asked me after putting me in a 'cell' (I mean cement blocks and all) for very disturbed

depressed patients (except I felt I was in some kind of prison for a crime I hadn't committed). The inhumanity there I found archaic. They asked me why I wasn't happy there.

Marilyn felt that at the very least, a psychiatrist from the hospital should have taken the trouble to talk to that institution's disturbed inmates:

> ... perhaps to alleviate even temporarily their misery and pain. I think they (the doctors) might learn something even—but all are only interested in something from the books they studied.

When the doctors told Marilyn how they prided themselves on the 'wall-to-wall carpeting and modern furniture' on the sixth floor of the hospital, she replied:

> Well, that any good interior decorator could provide—providing there are funds for it, but since they are dealing with human beings why couldn't they perceive even an interior of a human being. Oh, well, men are climbing to the moon but they don't seem interested in the beating human heart.[11]

Marilyn stated that, at Payne Whitney Hospital, she 'noticed there was no way of buzzing or reaching for a light to call the nurse'. When she asked the reason for this, she was told 'this is a psychiatric floor'. Whereupon, in exasperation, she 'picked up a light-weight chair and slammed it, and it was hard to do because [she] had never broken anything in [her] life—against the glass intentionally'.

When the medical staff arrived, she told them: 'if you are going to treat me like a nut I'll act like a nut':

> I indicated if they didn't let me out I would harm myself—the furthest thing from my mind at that moment since you know, Dr. Greenson, I'm an actress and would never intentionally mark or mar myself, I'm just that vain. Remember when I tried to do away with myself I did it very carefully with ten seconal and ten tuonal and swallowed them with relief (that's how I felt at the time).[12]

At about this time, Marilyn told Lee and Paula Strasberg: 'I know I will never be happy but I know I can be gay!'[13]

In late April 1961, Marilyn resumed psychotherapy under the care of Dr Greenson.

Despite her years of psychotherapy (which would finally total eight in all), it was Berniece's opinion that 'Marilyn had been stronger, healthier, and more self-confident before she went to New York.'[14] I.e., before she commenced her first course of psychotherapy.

# What Did These Various Psychoanalysts Make of Marilyn?

## Anna Freud
She stated of Marilyn as follows:

> Emotional instability, exaggerated impulsiveness, constant need for external approval, inability to be alone, tendency to depression in case of rejection, paranoid with schizophrenic elements.[15]

According to Jennifer Jean Miller, biographer of Marilyn and DiMaggio, the physician at Payne Whitney Psychiatric Clinic to which Marilyn was admitted in February 1961, stated that the latter 'was not schizophrenic, but "psychiatrically disconnected in an acute way" due to the stress of her last two films and [her] divorce'.[16]

## Ralph Greenson
To Anna Freud, Greenson described Marilyn as 'a sick, borderline, paranoid addict'.[17] To his friend, Lucille Ostrow, in mid-July 1962, Greenson described Marilyn as 'schizophrenic'.[18]

Susan Strasberg listed the numerous epithets that various people had attached to Marilyn in respect of her mental state: 'Schizophrenic, manic-depressive, paranoid, neurologically damaged, undergoing a spiritual crisis'.[19]

## Hyman Engelberg
> We knew that she was a manic depressive which is now called bi-polar personality disorder. I think the name manic depressive is better. It's more descriptive. That always meant there were emotional problems and that she could have big swings in her moods.[20]

So which, if any, of these various diagnoses was correct? This will be discussed shortly.

As for Marilyn, to Paula Strasberg she wrote the following undated note:

> Oh Paula I wish I knew why I am so anguished. I think maybe I'm crazy like all the other members of my family were, when I was sick I was sure I was. I'm so glad you are with me here![21]

In other words, for Marilyn, lurking in the background was always the fear that she herself, might be insane.

# Marilyn and Borderline Personality Disorder

As already mentioned, among the various diagnoses applied to Marilyn by psychiatrists and others were schizophrenia, bipolar disorder, and paranoia. Were any of them correct?

## Schizophrenia

For a significant amount of time during a one-month period, the subject experiences two or more of the following symptoms and signs:

> Delusions; hallucinations; disorganised speech (e.g., frequent derailment—thought disorder or speech containing a sequence of unrelated or only remotely related ideas—or incoherence); grossly disorganized or catatonic behaviour [i.e. decreased or excessive motor (muscular) activity]; negative symptoms (i.e., diminished emotional expression or avolition [lack of interest in becoming engaged in goal-orientated behaviour]).[1]

Continuous signs of the disturbance persist for at least six months, and during the disturbance, the subject's level of functioning is markedly reduced.

## Bipolar Disorder

Bipolar disorder is characterised by a manic episode—a distinct period of abnormally and persistently elevated, expansive, or irritable mood and goal-directed activity or energy, lasting at least a week and present most of the day, nearly every day. During this period, three or more of the following symptoms are present:

Inflated self-esteem or grandiosity; decreased need for sleep (e.g., feels rested after only 3 hours of sleep); more talkative than usual or pressure to keep talking; flight [rapid shifting] of ideas or subjective experience that thoughts are racing; distractibility; increase in goal-directed activity or psychomotor agitation; excessive involvement in activities that have a high potential for painful consequences.

The manic episode may have been preceded by, or may be followed by, a hypomanic episode of shorter duration, or by a major depressive episode.[2]

## Paranoia

A pattern of pervasive distrust and suspiciousness of others such that their motives are interpreted as malevolent.[3]

## Conclusion

In respect of Marilyn, none of the above symptomatological profiles, when taken as a whole for each disorder, rings entirely true. This is based upon her own description of her feelings, and upon what those close to her said and wrote about her.

## Borderline Personality Disorder

The following sub-headings represent various characteristics of Borderline Personality Disorder (BPD). The question is, is a diagnosis of BPD applicable to Marilyn?

*1. Identity disturbance, unstable self-image; a feeling of lacking a meaningful relationship, nurturing, and support; seeing one's self as bad or evil*

During the course of her life, Marilyn composed many poem-like texts. For example, in her notebook, *circa* 1951, she wrote as follows, indicating that she was totally lacking in self-esteem:

> Fear of giving me the lines new
> maybe won't be able to learn them
> maybe I'll make mistakes
> people will either think I'm no good or
> laugh or belittle me or think I can't act.
> Women looked stern and critical—

unfriendly and cold in general
afraid director won't think I'm any good.
remembering when I couldn't do a god
damn thing.
then trying to build myself up with the
fact that I have done things right that
were even good and have had moments
that were excellent but the bad is heavier
to carry around and feel have no confidence
depressed mad.[4]

In her notebook, in 1955 or 1956, she wrote:

why do I feel
this torture
or why do I feel less
of a human being than others
(always so [? sort] of felt in
a way that I'm sub-human
why
in other words
I'm the worst
why?)
even physically
I was always sure
some [thing] was wrong with
me there—afraid to
say where
but I know where[5]

When Susan Strasberg told Marilyn 'I'd do anything to be like you', the latter was shocked and replied, 'Ah, don't say that. I'd give anything to be like you. People respect you.'[6]

## 2. Feelings of emptiness: a feeling that one does not actually exist

In early 1956, during the filming of *Bus Stop*, Marilyn wrote to Lee Strasberg as follows:

> Thanks for letting Paula [Lee's wife] help me on the picture … she is the only really warm woman I've known. It's just that I get before camera and my concentration and everything I'm trying to learn leaves me. Then I feel like I'm not existing in the human race at all.[7]

### 3. Frantic efforts to avoid real or imagined abandonment

The manner in which Marilyn clung on to her various 'attachment figures' has already been described. However, despite all of her efforts to avoid abandonment, she concluded, in an undated note, as follows:

> Only parts of us will ever
> touch parts of others—
> one's own truth is just
> that really—one's own truth.
> We can only share the
> part that is within another's knowing acceptable
> so one
> is for the most part alone.[8]

*Circa* 1951, she wrote:

> Alone !!!!!
> I am alone—I am always
> alone
> no matter what.[9]

### 4. Bouts of anxiety: episodic dysphoria (defined as a state of unease or dissatisfaction)[10]

Said her first husband, James Dougherty:

> Norma Jean[e] was late for everything, chiefly because of that dressing process. She could spend an hour deciding what to wear and just as long bathing. Every move at such times was painfully slow. I told her, 'You know they're going to have to wait for you at your own funeral'.[11]

This would appear to indicate that Marilyn was over anxious about her appearance.

In a long note, typed by her in late 1943, Marilyn several times mentions her sense of insecurity. She also confessed: '[I have] taken my small insecurities and built them up into a nervous tension which although it had outlets was always present...'[12]

In autumn 1946, Marilyn told Berniece that she was dissatisfied with the shape of her hands. Furthermore, she declared: 'My ears are worse than my hands. See how thin they are on the tops? Like paper. I never wear my hair pulled back if I can avoid it'.[13]

In a note, composed *circa* 1955, Marilyn appears to be trying to reassure herself about her anxieties:

When I start to
feel suddenly depressed
what does it come from
(in reality) trace incidents
maybe to
ex past time—feeling guilty?
realize all the sensitivity
aspects. not being ashamed
of whatever I feel
don't dismiss
this lightly either
not regretting saying
what I've said if it
is really true to me.

Later in the poem, she describes how she must 'consciously make [an] effort to relax' and release her tension:

try to stop chain reaction
before it gets started if
it does start—don't worry
realize it be aware of it
consciously making the effort.[14]

Said Billy Wilder, who directed Marilyn in *The Seven Year Itch* (1955):

She defies gravity. She hasn't the vaguest conception of the time of the day. She arrives late and tells you she couldn't find the studio and [yet] she's been working there for years.[15]

Ezra Goodman described how Howard Hawks, who directed Marilyn in *Monkey Business* (1952) and *Gentlemen Prefer Blondes* (1953), 'told of how she showed up at 10:00 p.m. for a 9:00 p.m. date and explained: "I was here mentally at 9:00 p.m." Most people were of the opinion that Monroe's tardiness stemmed from her fear of facing up to any given situation.'[16]

So great was Marilyn's anxiety that she was unable to overcome it, no matter who she kept waiting.

In 1955 or 1956, she revealed that what she was most anxious about and what she feared most, was humiliation. Yet, she could not explain her feelings.

I feel guilty in as much as I know
what I'm saying what I'm and the (its)

effect—premeditated—except
I'm too inhibited
to feel spontaneous
I'm afraid
to be I mean—
because I don't
know what will
come out—what
will happen
even gas
off my stomach
(afraid to write fart)
and I will be
humiliated and
feel lower than
anything or anyone[17]

During the filming of *Something's Got to Give* (1962), her co-star Cyd Charisse said that when Marilyn 'was upstairs with Paula and she wouldn't come down if she didn't feel like she was ready for the scene. I think she had a lot of psychological problems.'[18]

## 5. Impulsivity, that is potentially damaging, including substance abuse, and being spendthrift.

It was Marilyn's habit, in times of stress or when she could not sleep, to reach for the pill bottle, and in early 1959, said Miller, she was increasingly dependent on, and incapacitated by drugs. However, he said: 'I had lost my faith in a lasting cure coming from me, and I wondered if indeed it could come from any human agency at all'.[19]

In 1960, said Berniece:

Marilyn began to come completely apart. By this time the medications Marilyn originally used to help her relax and sleep had turned against her and were changing her good-natured personality and affecting her ability to work.[20]

When Berniece visited Marilyn in July 1961, following the latter's gall bladder surgery, she noticed 'how many pills Marilyn consumes, and wishes that the doctor had prescribed nothing more habit forming than egg whites'.

Now that Marilyn had returned home she was taking as many pills as ever, 'maybe more. At home there were no nurses to supervise her'. Berniece asked the doctor when she would 'finally get off' the pills. Whereupon, Marilyn said sharply, 'I need those pills! I have to get my rest'.[21]

In late 1944, said Dougherty, following his 'trip around the world', he came home on leave:[22]

> [However, the] reason I went back to sea early: I ran out of money. I had left about a thousand dollars as our nest egg in the bank on my first trip home. When I looked at the bank book, it had all been drawn out. And she was spending nearly all of my allotment, about $170 a month.[23]

In 1946, during another period of leave, Dougherty discovered that Marilyn, who had filed for divorce 'had sold our silverware and pawned just about everything except the radio. Later, as Marilyn, she would run up huge bills at the Waldorf and other places and not really know where the money was coming from to pay them'.[24]

'Norma Jeane seems addicted to shopping', said Berniece in autumn 1946:

> [She] told me that she was supposed to save a percentage of her salary under contract. The Fox contract stipulated that she had to save it. That was standard for minors. But Norma Jeane spent all her salary anyway and didn't save anything.[25]

Marilyn did not 'comparison shop' (i.e. look for bargains) said Berniece in summer 1961:

> She just bought. She paid a hundred dollars for a dress that I would have paid ten for. To get her hair done cost her twenty-five to fifty dollars, when the going rate in a good shop in Manhattan was $12. And whatever anybody did for her, they charged her three times what they should have.[26]

As for charities, they 'continually begged for donations. If she didn't give, she'd get bad publicity, so she had to give to everybody who asked her. There was always somebody making her feel that she had to give money. And she gave it. She couldn't say no'.[27]

### 6. Instability in interpersonal relationships; may switch from idealizing other people, to devaluing them because they do not care enough or do not give enough

> Anger is often elicited when a caregiver or lover is seen as neglectful, withholding, uncaring, or abandoning.[28]

Writing in 1956, Goodman described how Marilyn often left people 'in the lurch'.

Monroe has a neat habit of latching on to people, of having them mother and father her, and then dumping them unceremoniously by the wayside when she has done with them. This goes for agents, drama coaches, columnists, lawyers, foster parents and just plain folk. She acquires them—and gets rid of them—in shifts. She likes to change people like other women change hats.

This is unfair to Marilyn in respect of her foster parents, for she had little or no control over who they were to be. Continued Goodman:

She got rid of her last coterie, consisting of agent Charles Feldman [head of the Famous Artists Agency], columnist-adviser Sidney Skolsky, drama coach Natasha Lytess and lawyer Frank Delaney, at one fell swoop and replaced them simultaneously with agent Lew Wasserman, photographer-adviser Milton Greene, drama coach Paula Strasberg and lawyer Irving Stein.[29]

Another person to 'bite the dust' was Loyd Wright, Monroe's West Coast lawyer, who was also given his notice.[30]

### 7. Inappropriate displays of anger: difficulty in controlling anger
Said Dougherty of Marilyn: 'There were moods in her that were unpredictable and often a little scary'.[31]

Susan Strasberg opined:

[Her father, Lee, was] the person with the key to free her [Marilyn] from her cage. I watched her fight harder and harder to keep her anger sedated with pills, drinks [i.e. alcoholic], or sexual exploits. She was trying to acknowledge her rebelliousness, resentment, frustration, guilt, self-hatred, instead of turning them against herself with erratic behavior or overdoses.[32]

### 8. Paranoia—i.e. delusions of persecution, unwarranted jealousy, or exaggerated self-importance.[33] Distrust and suspiciousness of others, whose motives are interpreted as malevolent.[34]

Marilyn herself confessed, *circa* 1973, when she was married to Dougherty, to having 'unfounded jealousies'.[35]

In 1995 or 1996, she wrote in her diary:

the feeling of violence I've had lately
about being afraid
of Peter he might
harm me,
poison me, etc.

why—strange look in his eyes—strange
behavior.

This was probably a reference to British-born actor Peter Lawford, who was a longstanding acquaintance of hers.[36, 37]

In spring 1962, Susan Strasberg said that her mother, Paula, had told her, in regard to Marilyn:

> It's different this time, Susie. It's different. I've never seen her like this, pulled in so many directions. She's running to psychics, afraid the Mafia is after her, that all her friends are using her [there was some truth in this]…[38]

## 9. Severe dissociative symptoms; becoming disconnected from one's thoughts, feelings, memories, or sense of identity

In her diary in 1955 or 1956, Marilyn declared that she loved Arthur Miller and trusted him. Yet, she continued:

> why is it I have
> a feeling—things are
> not really happening—but
> I'm playing a part… [39]

Taken singly, the various features of Marilyn's character, as outlined above, might be viewed as variations in 'normal' ideation (the formation of ideas) and behaviour. However, taken together, they point fairly conclusively to a diagnosis of Borderline Personality Disorder.[40] Yet there was one other feature of BPD that Marilyn possessed in abundance. It was by far the most serious, and for her, it would prove to be an existential threat.

## 10. Recurrent Suicidal Behaviour, Gestures, or Threats: Self-Mutilating Behaviour

Marilyn told George Carpozi that it was during the time of her marriage to James Dougherty that 'she made an attempt—although "not a very serious one"—at suicide'.[41]

In 1958, Marilyn wrote:

> After one year of analysis
> Help Help
> Help
> I feel life coming closer

when all I want
is to die[42]

In an undated note, Marilyn wrote:

Oh damn I wish that I were
Dead—absolutely nonexistent—
gone away from here—from
everywhere but how would I [do it]
There is always bridges—the Brooklyn
bridge...[43]

This was a reference to the Brooklyn Bridge, New York City, spanning the East River and connecting Manhattan to Brooklyn, a notorious suicide spot.

## Age of Onset of BPD

There is considerable variability in the course of borderline personality disorder. The most common pattern is one of chronic instability in early adulthood with episodes of serious affective and impulsive dyscontrol and high levels of the use of health and mental health resources.[44]

This fits with Marilyn, who, as already mentioned, made what was probably her first suicide attempt between the ages of sixteen and twenty, when she was married to Dougherty.

## Borderline Personality Disorder (BPD)

BPD was originally considered to be a disorder that is on the 'borderline' between neurosis and psychosis.

Neurosis: a mental disorder in which thought and emotions are so impaired that perception of external reality is severely affected.

Psychosis: a relatively mild mental illness not caused by organic disease, involving depression, anxiety, obsessive behaviour, etc., but not a radical loss of touch with reality.[45]

BPD is now considered to be a disorder in its own right. Although the term 'Borderline' goes no way to describing the condition adequately, nevertheless, in the absence of a better designation, the term has persisted.

# Arthur Miller:
## *After the Fall*

Marilyn's suicidal tendencies have already been alluded to. However, a play written by her third husband, Arthur Miller, appears to shed a chilling light on this aspect of her psyche.

Miller wrote his play, *After the Fall*, in 1962, the year after his divorce from Marilyn. Directed by Elia Kazan, it was first performed on 23 January 1964 at the ANTA (American National Theater and Academy), Washington Square Theatre, New York City, with Jason Robards Jr as Quentin, Barbara Loden as Maggie, and Salome Jens as Holga.

Due to the similarities between *After the Fall* and Miller's real-life marriage to Marilyn, it is certain beyond reasonable doubt that the play is largely, if not entirely, autobiographical.

Quentin is a New York, Jewish intellectual who has already been divorced twice; Arthur Miller was a divorcee when he married Marilyn.

Quentin is pondering over whether he should marry his most recent love, Holga, who is an archaeologist: 'I'm not sure, you see, if I want to lose her, and yet it's outrageous to think of committing myself again'.[1]

The first clue that this play is really about Marilyn is when Felice, a dancer and one time lover of Quentin, tells him, 'I had my nose fixed!'[2] Marilyn, too, underwent cosmetic surgery, designed to straighten her nose. Whereupon Quentin tells her that he 'liked her first nose better'.[3]

Says Quentin to Holga in respect of a possible future relationship between them: 'the doubt ties my tongue when I think of promising anything again'.[4] Maggie, Quentin's second wife, was a singer, who 'never really graduated high school', but 'always liked poetry'.[5] This also applies to Marilyn, in all three respects. However, she says, 'I'm a joke to most people'.[6]

In June 1962, having interviewed Marilyn, journalist Richard Meryman, declared:

[She is] a very anxious angry scared woman. I think she finally articulated her deep fear about herself and about this interview. I think she finally said it. 'Don't make me a joke'. I think she felt that on some level she was being treated as a joke.[7]

This was one of Marilyn's worst fears—that she would not be taken seriously, as an actress.

In an aside, Quentin says:

Fraud! From the first five minutes!... Because! I should have agreed she *was* a joke, a beautiful piece, trying to take herself seriously! Why did I lie to her, play this cheap benefactor...?[8]

This implies that Miller did not take Marilyn seriously, yet blamed himself for failing to be honest and tell her so.

When Quentin opines that Maggie's father must be proud of her, she replies: 'Oh, no—he left when I was eighteen months, see—'cause he said I wasn't from him, although my mother always said I was'.[9] This has echoes of Edward Mortensen, to whom Gladys was married at the time of her birth, and of Marilyn's biological father, Charles Stanley Gifford: '[However] he wouldn't even talk to me on the phone—just said 'See my lawyer', and hung up'.[10] This is allegedly what Marilyn herself was told, when she telephoned her own father, Gifford. Sensing that she is 'afraid to be alone here', Quentin asks 'why don't you call somebody to stay with you?' To this, Maggie replies, 'I don't know anybody ... like that'.

Quentin: 'Can I do anything? ... Don't be afraid to ask me.'[11]

Maggie tells Quentin: '[My mother] tried to kill me once with a pillow on my face 'cause I would turn out bad because of—like her sin'.[12] The possibility that Marilyn's mother Gladys did once attempt to suffocate her, for the reasons given above (even though *Time* magazine reported that the culprit was 'a demented neighbour'), though extremely unlikely, cannot be entirely discounted. After all, religion, to Gladys, was an overwhelming obsession.

Maggie: 'I love you, Quentin. I would do anything for you. And I would never bother you, I swear'.

Quentin: 'You're so beautiful it's hard to look at you'.[13]

Maggie asks Quentin: 'What do you see? Tell me! 'Cause I think ... you were ashamed once, weren't you?'

Quentin: 'I see your suffering, Maggie; and once I saw it, all shame fell away'.

Maggie: 'You... were ashamed!?'

Here, Miller may have been reflecting on the derogatory entry which he made about Marilyn in his diary, which she read, and the fallout from it.

Quentin: 'Yes. But you're a victory, Maggie, you're like a flag to me, a kind of proof, somehow, that people can win.[14] Look at the orchestra guys making a 'V' for victory! Everyone loves you, darling! Why are you sad?'[15]

Maggie: 'You love me?'

Quentin: 'I adore you. I just wish you could find some joy in your life'.

Maggie 'Quentin, I'm a joke that brings in money'.[16]

'I adore you, Maggie' says Quentin, [but] 'you need more love than I thought. But I've got it, and I'll make you see it, and when you do you're going to astound the world!'[17]

By now, Miller, for whom compassion is now his predominant feeling, has completely changed his tune in respect of Marilyn. Once, he despised her; now, he realises that despite all he loves her.

Maggie: 'I'm not a good wife. I take up so much of your work'.[18]

Quentin informs her that he keeps 'a log, I know what I spend my time on' and that he is 'putting in forty per cent of my time on your problems'.[19]

In other words, he appears to be agreeing with her.

When Maggie tells Quentin that she is 'not going to work tomorrow' he replies 'Okay'. Whereupon she says 'You know it's not "okay"! You're scared to death they'll sue me, why don't you say it?'[20] Twentieth Century Fox did once threaten to sue Marilyn, on 17 May 1962, during the filming of *Something's Got to Give*.

Quentin: 'you can't take pills on top of whisky, dear. That's how it happened the last time. And it's not going to happen again. Never'.[21]

Quentin dispossesses her of her tablets. Maggie tells him 'I was going to kill myself just now'. Did he not believe her? 'I saved you twice,' he replies. 'why shouldn't I believe it?'[22] As already mentioned, Angela Allen stated that, during the filming of *The Misfits* in 1960, Marilyn overdosed on two occasions.

Quentin: 'You want to die, Maggie, and I really don't know how to prevent it. But it struck me that I have been playing with your life out of some idiotic hope of some kind that you'd come out of this endless spell. But there's only one hope, dear— you've got to start to look at what *you're* doing'.

In other words, Miller believes that it is high time that Marilyn herself took responsibility for her actions.

Maggie asks Quentin if he intends 'to put me away somewhere'. He replies, 'You have to be supervised, Maggie'. She swallows some pills, whereupon he says, 'Now listen to me while you can still hear. If you start going under tonight [which presumably means lapsing into unconsciousness as a result of an overdose] I'm calling the ambulance'. She drinks some whisky and Quentin says, resignedly, 'Okay. I'll tell Carrie [Maggie's helper] to call the ambulance as soon as she sees the signs. I'm going to sleep at the inn'.[23]

Miller realises that the situation is hopeless, and for him, the stress is so great that he can no longer bear to sleep under the same roof as Marilyn.

Quentin confesses to Maggie: 'Yes, I lied. Every day. We are all separate people. I tried not to be, but finally one is—a separate person. I have to survive too, honey'.[24] In order to survive, Miller feels that he must hold on to his own identity.

In respect of her pills, Quentin tells Maggie:

You're trying to make me the one who does it to you? I grab them; and then we fight, and then I give them up, and you take your death from me. Something in you has been setting me up for a murder. Do you see it? But now I'm going away; so you're not my victim any more. It's just you, and your hand.[25]

Miller believes that Marilyn is trying to absolve herself of responsibility, and instead lay the blame on him for her intended suicide.

Quentin remonstrates with her saying, 'Let's keep it true—you told me you tried to die long before you met me'.[26] Here, Quentin is surely echoing Miller's own, real-life thoughts—i.e. that it was unfair of Marilyn to blame him, because she had attempted suicide even before they first became acquainted.

Maggie: 'You were ashamed of me.... That's what killed me, Quentin!'
 Quentin: 'All right. I wasn't ... ashamed. But ... afraid'.[27] He reminds Maggie that she had once described him as 'cold, remote'.
 Maggie: 'Don't mix me up with Louise [his first wife]!'
 Quentin: That's just it. That I could have brought two women so different to the same accusation—it closed a circle for me. And I wanted to face the worst thing I could imagine—that I could not love. And I wrote it down, like a letter from hell'.[28]

Having had two unsuccessful marriages, Miller now regarded himself as a failure, and, to his deep regret, as a person who was incapable of love.

Quentin: 'It isn't my love you want any more. It's my destruction!'[29] He believes that she is now trying to destroy him. Maggie and Quentin have a fight, as he attempts to take the bottle of pills from her. He grabs her by the throat before falling back 'in horror'.

Says Maggie triumphantly: 'Now we both know. You tried to kill me, mister. I've been killed by a lot of people, some couldn't hardly spell, but it's the same, mister. You're on the end of a long, long line'.[30] It appears that Marilyn placed the blame for all her previous suicidal attempts and suicidal notions on those who intervened to save her life?

Was *After the Fall* a work of pure fiction? Hardly, for the reasons outlined above. Rather, it appears to be both autobiographical, on Miller's part, and highly revealing about his married life with Marilyn. The author Thomas Hardy, it will be remembered, wrote dozens of poems in memory of his late wife, and although Miller's wife was not deceased, but divorced from him when he wrote his play, it seems virtually certain that, for both men, it was a catharsis, and a means of trying to make sense of the seemingly unintelligible events of the past.

Finally, what *After the Fall* reveals, above all, is that Marilyn's desire to take her own life was powerful, of long standing, and irreversible.

# Mental Disorders in the Family:
# The Origin of Marilyn's Condition

### Tilford Marion Hogan (Marilyn's Maternal Great-Grandfather)

Tilford committed suicide in May 1933. He was in poor health, and as a farmer, he had been ruined by the Great Depression.

### Otis Elmer Monroe (Marilyn's Maternal Grandfather)

Otis died in the California State Hospital for the mentally ill in July 1909. The diagnosis was 'general paresis'—i.e. general paralysis of the insane. This is the result of neurological syphilis, in which chronic meningoencephalitis leads, in the terminal phase of this disease, to cerebral atrophy.

### Della May Monroe (Marilyn's Maternal Grandmother)

When Della was admitted to Norwalk State Hospital, where she died in August 1927, the doctors made a diagnosis of 'manic depressive psychosis' and 'myocarditis'. Yet to what extent her symptoms were occasioned by the malaria, from which, according to Marilyn, she was currently suffering, is not known.

### Gladys (Marilyn's Mother)

Aside from Gladys' hospital records, which are largely inaccessible, by far the most important account of her mindset is contained in a document composed by Grace Goddard in about 1952. Gladys was then aged about fifty. It ends, 'I wrote these things down as Gladys said them while she was staying with me',

*Making Sense of Marilyn*

and it is signed 'Grace Goddard'.[1] The account, as will now be seen, points to the following abnormalities in Gladys's thought processes:

## Delusions

Delusion: an idiosyncratic belief or impression that is not in accordance with a generally accepted reality.[2]

> Because she, Gladys had trouble on last nursing job, [this] led her to go and get a ballot on socialism and study it.
> [She] thinks she was sent to State Hospital because years ago she voted on a Socialist Ballot at Hawthorne and was being punished for doing so.
> She thinks she was a nurse working for the Govt. while in Agnew, and thinks she should apply to the Government for a job in the Army to be sent overseas.
> [Believes that she] never needed to be sent to Norwalk or Agnew as she had her nervous breakdown after being sent to Agnew.
> She is confused now because <u>once</u> she took an aspirin when she lived with Stewart [John Stewart Eley].
> No one should listen to Radio Broadcasts because the people who are behind them are all drunkards and everyone on the radio are drunk when they go on the air.
> Thinks she can vote on both Republican and Democratic ballots.
> She is being punished because years ago she took a drink of liquor (during prohibition) and should have been sent to jail.
> Blames her confused conditions on unions.

## Religious Mania

> Wishes she never had had a sexual experience so she could be more Christ like.

## Paranoia

> She has a fear of Catholics. Every time she attends Christian Science church, instead of listening to the Readers, she spends her time mentally protecting herself from the thought that a Catholic or someone of another (than CS) Protestant Denomination, who might be in the Congregation trying to harm her.
> Misplaces or losing her glasses, watch, gloves or other possessions and either accuses some one of stealing them, or are to blame for her losing them.

In addition, Gladys exhibited diminished emotional expression, catatonic behaviour (i.e. arising from a disturbed mental state), disorganised behaviour (reduced ability to care for herself, work, or interact with others) avolition.

Finally, the above and the fact that Gladys exhibited these abnormal features in her early thirties (at or before January 1934, when she was admitted to Santa Monica Asylum at the age of thirty-two), all support the diagnosis of schizophrenia—the peak age of onset for this disease being, for females, the late twenties.

This was the conclusion arrived at by the medical staff of Norwalk State Hospital in January 1935. They diagnosed 'paranoid schizophrenia' in Gladys, as already mentioned.

## Marilyn's Paternal Ancestors

Of the forebears of Marilyn's father Charles Stanley Gifford, little is known.

## Marilyn herself

Borderline Personality Disorder (BPD) affects between 1.6 and 5.9 per cent of the population, and it is about five times more common in first-degree biological relatives of those with the disorder, than in the general population.[3] (In Marilyn's case, this means parents, as she had no offspring, and only half-siblings.) The question therefore arises, did any of Marilyn's relations have BPD? The answer, as far as is known, is no.

# Something's Got to Give

The film *Something's Got to Give*, starring Marilyn, Dean Martin, and Cyd Charisse, was to be produced by Twentieth Century Fox.

On 10 April 1962, Marilyn appeared on set for make-up and costume tests (photographs that allow the filmmakers and designers to get a clear idea of colours, fabrics, and styles). However, that evening, when Marilyn was several hours late for an appointment, Henry T. Weinstein, one of the films co-producers, hurried over to her home at nearby Brentwood where he found her unconscious. He said, 'I come there and she's spread across her bed practically nude and really out.' It was a well-known habit of Marilyn's to drink champagne with her sleeping tablets, but this time, the combination of the two had resulted in an overdose.[1]

Weinstein immediately summoned Dr Ralph Greenson, her psychiatrist, and Dr Hyman Engleberg, her general physician for help. Film taken after Marilyn had been revived, show her, uncharacteristically, turning her face away from the camera and holding her head in her hands.[2]

Filming commenced on 23 April 1962. Marilyn, however, did not appear on the set until 30 April because, at the commencement of filming, she 'had a virus and a sinus infection'. Nonetheless, said Berniece, she 'has high hopes' that not only the current film, *Something's Got to Give*, but also its successor, *What a Way to Go*, in which she was also scheduled to star, would be 'completed according to schedule'. If so, by spring 1963, she would have fulfilled her commitment to Fox and, thereafter, 'be a free agent'.[3]

The opening scene of the film is a courtroom where Ellen (Marilyn), the wife of Nick (Dean Martin), who had been lost at sea five years previously, is pronounced to be legally deceased. Nick now announces that he intends to remarry, whereupon the judge marries him on the spot to Bianca (Cyd Charisse). However, Ellen now reappears on the scene, and the inevitable complications ensue.

At the time of filming, said Berniece, although Marilyn's physician (Dr Hyman Engelberg) 'was supposedly easing her off medication ... she was taking chloral hydrate as a sleeping sedative'.[4]

On 1 May 1962, Marilyn arrived on the film set at 7 a.m., but shortly afterwards collapsed and was sent home.

On 17 May 1962, with the permission of producer Henry Weinstein, Marilyn left the film set in order to sing at a celebration to be held at Madison Square Garden, Manhattan, on 19 May in honour of President John F. Kennedy's forty-fifth birthday. (The President's actual forty-fifth birthday was ten days later, on 29 May.) Marilyn was here at the invitation of John F. Kennedy's brother-in-law actor, Peter Lawford, who, on 24 April 1954, had married Patricia Kennedy, the President's sister. Following her 'split' with husband, Arthur Miller, in January 1961, said Barris, Marilyn had embarked upon a relationship with President Kennedy. This he described as a 'serious romance'.

Marilyn was introduced, jokingly, as 'the late Marilyn Monroe'—a reference to her habitual lateness. However, this was to prove ironic in view of the fate that was shortly to befall her. Marilyn sang 'Happy Birthday', in a voice that was slow, laboured, and husky: her body hunched over the microphone; her eyes downcast; and her face pinched and drawn.

Said George Barris:

> ... the President's wife had not been invited, and Marilyn had a Cinderella fantasy that Kennedy would divorce Jackie and marry her, that she would then become First Lady. Instead, it is rumoured the President passed her on to his kid brother Bobby, and after a while this romance soured, too. She never forgave the Kennedy brothers, feeling she had been just another of their rich boy's playthings.[5]

Following her 'split' with husband, Arthur Miller, in January 1961, said Barris, Marilyn had embarked upon a relationship with President Kennedy. This, he described as a 'serious romance'.

On 22 May 1962, Marilyn had another three days of absence, when she refused to work with Dean Martin because he was suffering from a cold. After four weeks of production, she had been present on set for only a few days, and by 29 May, the film was eleven days behind schedule. Marilyn, however, was able to laugh when she forgot her lines, and Dean Martin was very supportive.

When film director George Cukor asked Marilyn if she would agree to perform the swimming-pool scene in the nude, she agreed, and on 23 May, the nude swimming scene was duly filmed.[6] On 27 and 28 May, Marilyn was indisposed due to an ear infection.

On 1 June 1962 (which was Marilyn's thirty-sixth birthday) filming resumed, and this time she did remember her lines. Said George Barris: 'I think she realized, you know, I'm going to be thirty six and thirty seven, thirty eight, and there's a lot of new girls coming along who could replace me'.[7]

At 6 p.m., Marilyn's birthday cake was brought out and her birthday party began. She rounded the day off by attending a function in aid of the Muscular Dystrophy Foundation.

On 4 June 1962, Marilyn was once again too ill to work. In fact, she had worked for only thirteen of thirty production days, and the film was over budget. An angry James Dean now walked off the set.

On 8 June, Marilyn was officially fired by Fox. However, when Lee Remick was chosen to replace her, Dean Martin resigned. On 11 June, the entire cast and crew were put on suspension—104 people in all. In the meantime, said Berniece, Marilyn was interviewed and participated in 'cover photography sessions' for various magazines, including *Vogue, Cosmopolitan*, and *Life* (which featured an article about her). She now approached Cyd Charisse and asked her if she would be prepared to restart filming. Cyd said yes, of course she would.

In the period 29 June to 1 July 1962, Marilyn fulfilled an appointment with Barris, who declared:

> Marilyn was often late for our photo sessions. One day I waited for her for what seemed like hours, when suddenly she appeared on the beach with a strange-looking hairdresser and an even stranger-looking make-up man; the car was filled with clothes. I knew she never travelled with an entourage, so these two had to be her faithful friends, Agnes Flanagan and Allan 'Whitey' Snyder, who were constantly at Marilyn's beck and call.[8]

Nevertheless, in that month of June, Marilyn told Barris: 'As far as I'm concerned, the happiest time of my life is now. There's a future, and I can't wait to get to it. It should be interesting'.[9]

That summer, she also told Barris: 'I'm just getting started. I'd like to be a fine actress—comedy, tragedy interspersed'. She also professed an interest in horticulture, and in the arts.[10]

On 12 July 1962, Marilyn was reinstated by Fox; Dean Martin having refused to participate in the film without her being present.[11] According to her new agreement with Fox, Paula Strasberg would be barred from the set and director George Cukor, would be replaced by Romanian-US film director and screenwriter Jean Negulesco. Meanwhile, said Berniece, she 'has frequent appointments with Dr Greenson and her physician Dr Engelberg for an ongoing virus'.[12]

It was on Santa Monica beach, California, on 13 July 1962 at 'around 7:30 p.m.', said Barris, that he took his last ever photograph of Marilyn.[13]

It was Barris, who gave a shrewd analysis of the various *dramatis personae* in Marilyn's life, under various headings. For example:

| | |
|---|---|
| Friend: | Paula Strasberg, drama coach, Svengali; Natasha Lytess, drama coach, Svengali. |
| Confidante: | Susan Strasberg, actress, confidante. |
| Questionable friend: | John Huston, movie director. |
| No friend: | Joan Crawford, actress, acquaintance; Tony Curtis, actor, acquaintance; Otto Preminger, film director. |
| User: | Eunice Murray, housekeeper; Laurence Olivier, actor, director. |
| No friend; user: | George Cukor, director; Darryl Zanuck, Fox Studio chief. |
| Heart breaker; user: | John F. Kennedy, United States president; Robert F. Kennedy, United States attorney general.[14] |

It was noticeable in sections of the film *Something's Got to Give*—which were released subsequently—that Marilyn's facial mannerisms were still there, as she opened and closed her mouth with her lips apart, or blew upwards towards a lock of her hair that was overlying her forehead. Yet while the mouth smiled, the eyes lacked their former sparkle, and she bore a quizzical, somewhat vacant look. However, although she looked washed out, with drooping eyelids and a flat expression, she did burst out laughing when filming a scene with an uncooperative dog, which romped about climbing up on her shoulders and licking her ear.[15]

On 1 August 1962, Marilyn signed her new contract with Fox for the film *Something's Got to Give*, for which she would be paid the sum of $250,000. However, before filming could resume, fate would intervene.

On Friday 3 August 1962, said Berniece, Marilyn telephoned her lawyer, Milton Rudin, and made an appointment for the following Monday 6 August 'to make revisions in her will'. She also arranged for her dress designer to attend her at her home on the same day, and to meet songwriter Jule Styne the following Thursday (9 August) in New York, where she would be staying with the Strasbergs. Finally, she spoke to Norman Rosten, and told him that 'she hopes to see him and [his wife] Hedda while she is in New York'.

She went to a session with psychiatrist Dr Greenson in his office, and she visited Arthur Jacobs' office to view a film directed by Lee Thompson. She decided to meet Thompson, and the meeting was arranged for Monday 6 August at 5 p.m. She also telephoned Peter Lawford and arranged to visit Washington DC on 27 September to attend the world premiere of the Irving Berlin musical *Mr President* with him and his wife, Patricia.[16]

Meanwhile, in the late afternoon of 3 August 1962, said Barris, he received a phone call from Marilyn. She asked him about the magazine story he was writing about her and their 'book project'. He stated: '…both were going well. There's so much more I want to tell you for the book'. 'When are you coming back?' she enquired—i.e., from New York City to LA. She proceeded to tell Barris, excitedly, how Jack Benny 'wanted her to put together a Las Vegas show with him'. Also, Frank Sinatra and Marlon Brando 'had called with film offers, and a top producer had offered her a starring role in a Broadway play (something else she'd always dreamed of). Fox wanted her to begin shooting a film with Dean Martin in September'.

'You've just got to get back here,' she said. Her voice sounded like she had just hit the jackpot. She never seemed happier.

Following this, Barris told Marilyn that he would try to leave by Monday, or at least by the middle of the week. She closed by saying, 'Love you—see you Monday or when you get out here'.[17]

Marilyn described Brando as her favourite motion-picture star and said, in the context of the two of them making a film together, 'I believe we'd be an interesting combination'.[18]

Brando stated that he had first met Marilyn 'briefly, shortly after the war'—i.e. in the late 1940s. The two met again at the Actors Studio after the filming of *A Streetcar Named Desire* (released September 1951, in which he starred with Vivien Leigh). 'While the other people at the party drank and danced, she sat by herself almost unnoticed in a corner, playing the piano'. Brando continued:

> Marilyn was a sensitive, misunderstood person, much more perceptive than was generally assumed. She had been beaten down, but had a strong emotional intelligence—a keen intuition for the feelings of others, the most refined type of intelligence. After that first visit, we had an affair and saw each other intermittently until she died in 1962.

Brando was of the opinion that '[Lee] Strasberg and other people were trying to use her'.[19]

Brando's experiences of life were similar, in many respects, to those of Marilyn herself. He spoke about his loneliness, and being brought up in a 'friendless household'.[20] He also spoke of his emotional insecurity as a child: '... of wanting love and not being able to get it, of realizing that I was of no value'.[21]

The following statement by Brando is one with which Marilyn would surely have empathised: 'I have always been suspicious of success, it's pitfalls and how it can undo you'.[22]

Like Marilyn, Brando was concerned for the poor and underprivileged: for example, the oppressed African-Americans in the US and victims of famine in India. Like Marilyn, he supported many charitable causes. Finally, Brando also suffered a nervous breakdown and was under the care of psychiatrists 'for many years'.[23]

To return to Marilyn, on the evening of Friday 3 August, Dr Engelberg paid her a visit and gave her an injection 'to help her sleep and, because the chloral hydrate has apparently not been working, writes her a prescription for twenty five Nembutal capsules'.[24]

That same evening, 'Pat Newcomb arrives at Marilyn's house to spend the night.'[25] It was Pat, said Barris, 'who handled Marilyn's press and acted as her major-domo. Part of Marilyn's "family", Pat handled Marilyn's wardrobe and her fans, but was much more than an employee; she was a best friend. She was ten years younger than Marilyn'.[26]

On the night of Saturday 4 August, said Berniece, Dr Greenson visited Marilyn 'at about 5:00 p.m. and spends an hour talking in the bedroom' with her. She declined supper 'as she had declined lunch'.[27]

That same evening, said Dr Engleberg, Marilyn received several telephone calls, including one from Joe DiMaggio Junior, her former stepson.[28]

# Death of Marilyn

## Events of the Night of the Saturday 4 to Sunday 5 August 1962

Dr Hyman Engelberg stated:

> I happened to talk to her on the phone that night, earlier in the evening, and she was happy and in a manic phase so I thought her mental state was good. She sounded cheerful. Apparently something happened to suddenly depress her.[1]
>
> I had prescribed, I think, twenty four Nembutal [for Marilyn's insomnia] which is a good dose, and of course she was supposed to take a few every night, but even if she took all at once, it's problematic that that was a fatal dose. We tried to keep it down and give her the Nembutal more frequently in smaller amounts.[2]

Eunice Murray, Marilyn's housekeeper, stated that, at about 9 p.m., 'Marilyn came to her bedroom door. I was sitting in the living room. She said, "Goodnight, Mrs Murray. I think I'll turn in now."'

At this point, she retired to her bedroom and 'closed the door'. Later that evening, said Dr Engelberg:

> Peter Lawford got a call from Marilyn and she was mumbling. Apparently she was going under from the pills she took. Perhaps this was a cry for help. He [Lawford] didn't run over. He called Milton Rudin [Marilyn's attorney] to tell him that Marilyn sounded funny, and would Milton check and call the housekeeper. At about 10 p.m. Rudin called Eunice Murray, who assured him that Marilyn was fine.

However, at about 3.30 a.m., Mrs Murray awoke and noticed the light was still on in Marilyn's bedroom. She said: 'I went around to the front of the house. Turning the curtain back [presumably by reaching through the open window], I saw Marilyn lying on the bed nude and I was just alarmed.'[3]

Dr Engelberg continued:

> Dr Greenson got there first. She was dead when he got there, and I went into the bedroom to make sure she was dead. There was some rigor mortis, yes, but it wasn't extreme yet, I suspected that she'd been dead at least a few hours.[4]
>
> At the side of her bed, there was a lot of Seconal which I had never given her. Also, the autopsy showed that her liver had a lot of chloral hydrate. I never gave her chloral hydrate and I don't think any doctor in the United States gave it to her. She must have bought it in Tijuana [a city in Mexico, near the border with California].[5]

## Plans for the Funeral

Inez Melson, Marilyn's business manager and Gladys's guardian since 1952, was interviewed by British film critic Barry L. Norman for the television series *The Hollywood Greats*. She stated:

> Because Marilyn had always said to me, when every once in a while someone in the film world would pass away and there would be mobs of people all wanting to see what was going on, she said, 'I hope that would never happen to me'.

Although it was Joe DiMaggio who selected Marilyn's casket, said Inez: 'I selected the guest list and I invited people that were not in the film industry at all, old friends'.[6]

Thirty relatives and friends attended the funeral, including Lee and Paula Strasberg, Dr Greenson and his family, and Grace Goddard's sister, Enid Knebelkamp, together with Enid's husband, Sam, and their daughter, Diane.

Frank Sinatra, Ella Fitzgerald, Peter Lawford, and Sammy Davis Jr all wished for a memorial service to be held for Marilyn, said Inez, but '[Inez] knew Marilyn didn't want a memorial service, so [he] refused permission for this to happen'.[7]

When Arthur Jacobs, founder of public relations company Arthur P. Jacobs, complained to Inez that, by her refusal, she was 'insulting the sister of the President of the United States'—Peter Lawford's wife, Patricia—she replied firmly, 'This isn't a political rally, this is the death of a very dear friend'.[8]

## The Funeral

Marilyn's funeral service was held on Wednesday 8 August 1962 at 1 p.m. at Westwood Village Memorial Park Cemetery, Los Angeles, California. (This was also the final resting place of Ana Lower and of Ana's niece, Grace Goddard.)

Leaving aside the controversy over the teaching methods of Lee Strasberg, the funeral eulogy that he delivered on the sad day was truly moving and entirely apposite. He described Marilyn as 'a warm human being, impulsive and shy, sensitive and in fear of rejection, yet ever avid for life and reaching out for fulfillment':

> When she first came to me I was amazed at the startling sensitivity which she possessed and which had remained fresh and undimmed, struggling to express itself despite the life to which she had been subjected. Others were as physically beautiful as she was, but there was obviously something more in her, something that people saw and recognized in her performances and with which they identified. She had a luminous quality—a combination of wistfulness, radiance, yearning—to set her apart and yet make everyone wish to be part of it, to share in the childish naivety which was at once so shy and yet so vibrant.
>
> This quality was even more evident when she was on the stage. I am truly sorry that the public who loved her did not have the opportunity to see her as we did, in many of the roles that foreshadowed what she would have become. Without a doubt she would have been one of the really great actresses of the stage.[9]

In his latter statement, Strasberg was mistaken, for as already mentioned, Marilyn could never have succeeded on the stage simply because she could not remember her lines.

As he sat in the rear seat of the car and was driven away from the funeral, the look of sadness on Joe DiMaggio's face was haunting and unforgettable. Gladys did not attend her funeral, neither did her former husbands, James Dougherty and Arthur Miller.

Marilyn was entombed in the Westwood Village Memorial Park Cemetery.

## Cause of Death

According to her death certificate, the cause of Marilyn's death was 'Acute Barbiturate Poisoning' and 'Ingestion of Overdose'.

The autopsy had been conducted by Deputy Coroner for Los Angeles County Dr Thomas Noguchi, who was joined by John Miner, Deputy District Attorney. Also present was Chief Medical Examiner-Coroner, County of Los Angeles, Dr Theodore Curphey.

Toxicology tests were performed on 6 August 1962 by R. L. Abernethy, toxicologist for the LA County Coroner. They revealed that Marilyn's bloodstream contained an 8-milligram percentage (mg%) of chloral hydrate and a 4.5-mg% of pentobarbital. Marilyn's liver contained a 13-mg% of pentobarbital. In regard to toxicity, the amount of chloral hydrate was below the lethal level of 25 mg%. However, the amount of pentobarbital was equivalent to a lethal dose: the potential lethal level being within the range of 1 mg% and 16.9 mg%.[10] Marilyn's other organs were not tested for drugs.

## Conspiracy Theories

Andrew Bevan, features director of *Teen Vogue & Style* magazine, stated:

> There's always going to be conspiracy theories about any famous person dying, and there's been rumors that the Mafia was involved, and the Kennedys, and the American Government, and the C.I.A. Its a lot easier to blame it on the C.I.A., or something like that, because this thirty-six-year-old beautiful talented actress is gone, than to just blame it on a senseless act of despair.[11]

## Was Marilyn's Death Suicide?

James Dougherty believed not. Had this been the case, he said, he was 'positive that Norma Jean[e] would have written a short note, telling the world 'good-bye,' if nothing else'.[12]

Arthur Miller, in a letter to his attorney and friend Joseph 'Joe' L. Rauh, stated that he did not believe Marilyn had taken her life intentionally: '[Although] I'd always worried that she'd step over the line,' he said, 'I don't think she meant to'.[13]

Joe DiMaggio blamed the film industry and the press for driving Marilyn to her death.

Berniece Miracle was convinced that Marilyn's death was 'definitely not suicide'. She said: 'I have never believed that Marilyn deliberately took her own life. She was too excited about the things she was doing. Especially her new home'.[14]

Dr Engelberg stated:

> I believe that she was in a manic phase, and that something happened to suddenly depress her and she grabbed pills. She had plenty of pills at the bedside. I think she was suddenly depressed and in that sense it was intentional. Then, I think she felt better of it when she felt herself going under, because she called Peter Lawford, so while it was intentional at the time, I do believe that she changed her mind.[15]

## Conclusions of the Suicide Prevention Center

On 14 August 1962, Dr Theodore Curphey stated:

> Marilyn Monroe died on the night of August 4, or the early morning of August 5, 1962. Examination by the toxicology laboratory indicates that death was due to a

self-administered overdose of sedative drugs. We have been asked, as consultants, to examine the life situation of the deceased and to give an opinion, regarding the intent of Miss Monroe when she ingested the sedative drugs which caused her death. From the data obtained, the following points are the most important and relevant.

Miss Monroe had suffered from psychiatric disturbance for a long time. She experienced severe fears and frequent depression. Mood changes were abrupt and unpredictable. Among symptoms of disorganization, sleep disturbance was prominent, for which she had been taking sedative drugs for many years. She was thus familiar with and experienced in the use of sedative drugs, and well aware of their dangers.

Recently, one of the main objectives of her psychiatric treatment had been the reduction of her intake of drugs. This has been partially successful during the last two months. She was reported to be following doctor's orders in her use of the drugs, and the amount of drugs found in her home at the time of her death was not unusual.

In our investigation, we have learned that Miss Monroe had often expressed wishes to give up, to withdraw, and even to die. On more than one occasion in the past, when disappointed and depressed, she had made suicide attempts using sedative drugs. On these occasions she had called for help and had to be rescued.

From the information collected about the events of the evening of August 4th, it is our opinion that the same pattern was repeated, except the rescue. It had been our practice with similar information collected in other cases in the past to recommend a certification for such deaths as probable suicide.

Additional clues for suicide provided by the physical evidence are: 1) the high level of barbiturates and chloral hydrate in the blood which, with other evidence from the autopsy, indicates the probable ingestion of a large amount of the drugs within a short period of time: 2) the completely empty bottle of Nembutal, the prescription for which was filed the day before the ingestion of the drugs: 3) the locked door which was unusual.

On the basis of all information obtained, it is our opinion that the case is a probable suicide.[16]

## Adverse Effects of Drugs

### Barbiturates (including Nembutal and Seconal)

Barbiturates are prescription central nervous system depressants. They are often used and abused in the search for a sense of relaxation, or a desire to 'switch off' or forget stress-related thoughts or feelings.

However, they are likely to be habit-forming and have long since been replaced by safer medicines for the treatment of insomnia. Signs and symptoms of recent use can include:

Drowsiness
Slurred speech
Lack of coordination
Euphoria or an exaggerated feeling of well-being
Problems concentrating or thinking
Memory problems
Involuntary eye movements (nystagmus)
Lack of inhibition
Slowed breathing and reduced blood pressure
Dizziness
Depression[17]

Nembutal (sodium pentobarbitone) is used for the short-term treatment of insomnia. Possible side effects are impaired memory and cognition, and physical or psychological dependence.

Seconal (secobarbital) is used in the short term to treat insomnia. It can be habit forming.

## Chloral Hydrate

Chloral hydrate is a non-barbiturate sedative that slows down the central nervous system and brain activity, causing extreme drowsiness and deep sleep within an hour, depending on the dosage.

Chloral hydrate can be prescribed as a short-term sleeping pill for two to seven days. Using it for more than a week can cause addiction. Another risk of chloral hydrate is that it is relatively easy to overdose and die. A combination of chloral hydrate and alcohol may produce intoxication and unconsciousness.

Symptoms of a chloral hydrate drug overdose are most often low body temperature and coma. Some people appear drunk in that they will have slurred speech, extreme drowsiness, and confusion. Other symptoms can be difficulty breathing, weakness, slow heartbeat, nausea, extreme drowsiness, fainting, uneven (irregular) heartbeat, and muscle weakness.[18]

Chloral hydrate is taken orally for the short-term treatment of insomnia. It may cause disorientation as a side effect.

There is no doubt that Marilyn was addicted to barbiturates and probably to other drugs and that she frequently took a combination of drugs and alcohol-containing drinks. In respect of the potential side effects of the aforementioned drugs, it was noticeable that, during the latter stages of her career, her speech was often slurred and she often appeared to be drowsy and uncoordinated. The barbiturates, in particular, may well have exacerbated her depression, which was a feature of her BPD.

# Epilogue

The film *What a Way to Go*, in which Marilyn would have appeared but for her sudden demise, was released on 2 July 1964, with Shirley MacLaine fulfilling the role that had been intended for Marilyn.

## Gladys

'She didn't seem to have the slightest reaction to the fact that Marilyn had just died,' said Berniece when she visited Gladys at Rockhaven Sanitarium to tell her the sad news.[1]

When Berniece asked Gladys why, despite the fact that she had not wanted her daughter to become an actress, she had named her after 'movie stars', Gladys replied: 'That is a lie! I did not. I named her after Norma Jeane Cohen in Louisville Kentucky'.[2] This was evidently a reference by Gladys to Norma Jean— note spelling—Cohen of Louisville, who, on 6 May 1941, married Leon Seidman. Whether she and Gladys were acquainted is not known.[3]

Under the terms of Marilyn's will, $5,000 per annum was allocated 'for the maintenance and support of [her] mother Gladys Baker, during her lifetime'.[4] However, because of a delay in the granting of probate by the court, Marilyn's bequest of monies for her mother's care could not immediately be implemented.

In 1963, Gladys absconded from Rockhaven Sanatarium but was apprehended. On 27 April 1966, she was transferred to Camarillo State (Mental) Hospital, Camarillo, California. In 1967, 'after she attempted suicide,' said Berniece, 'I took custody of her.' Probate was eventually granted in 1977, when 'the trust fund for Gladys becomes active'.[5]

Gladys died in Collins Court home for the elderly, Gainesville, Florida on 11 March 1984, aged eighty-one.[6]

# Marilyn's Former Husbands

Having discussed Marilyn's death with his brother, Tom, James Dougherty declared:

> We both agreed that she had needed a more secluded life, a more protected life, with people who were sincerely her friends, like the many friends she had when we were married, neighbors, family.[7]
>
> From a distance, I knew that she was making an effort to change her image, to be accepted finally as a real actress. But she must have felt frustrated in this because in that little scene I saw from her last, unfinished movie, she seemed to be back where she was ten years earlier—a dumb blond sexpot.[8]

Following his divorce from Marilyn, Dougherty was married twice more: first to Pat Scoman in 1947 and second to Rita Lambert in 1974. He retired from the LAPD in 1974 after twenty-five years' service. Dougherty died on 15 August 2005, aged eighty-four.

After Marilyn's death her second husband Joe DiMaggio, was 'heartbroken', said Inez Melson.[9] Subsequently, the following note was found in Marilyn's bedroom, addressed to him:

> Dear Joe
>
> If I can only succeed in making you happy—I will have succeeded in the big[g]est and most difficult thing there is—that is to make one person completely happy. Your happiness means my happiness, and...[10]

The note ended abruptly.

DiMaggio's final gift to Marilyn was a twice-weekly present of six roses, in perpetuity.[11] They were to be placed in a vase attached to the front of her tomb, beside the simple inscription:

MARILYN MONROE

1926–1962

Following his divorce from Marilyn, DiMaggio did not remarry. He died on 8 March 1999, aged eighty-four.

Marilyn's third husband, Arthur Miller declared:

> [For many weeks after Marilyn's death] I found myself having to come about and force myself to encounter the fact that Marilyn had ended. I realized that I still,

even then, expected to meet her once more, somewhere, sometime, and maybe talk sensibly about all the foolishness we had been through—in which case I would probably have fallen in love with her again.[12]

Following his divorce from Marilyn, Miller married Inge Morath in 1962. He died on 10 February 2005, aged eighty-nine.

## George Barris

Only days before he was due to meet her in Los Angeles, Barris was told that Marilyn had died. His telephone 'kept ringing all night long' he said. 'Friends were calling—more press', but he 'had nothing to say'.[13] In other words, he was too distressed to speak.

On 8 August 1962, the London *Daily Mirror* commenced a series of features about Marilyn, which 'ran for four days,' said Barris. On 14 August 1962, the *New York Daily News* commenced a feature about Marilyn which 'ran for a full week. Each newspaper had the largest circulation in its [respective] country'.[14]

In order 'to escape the pressure' from the press, which 'was constantly hounding me for interviews about Marilyn,' said Barris, 'I fled to Paris.' Here he remained for over twenty years until returning to the US with his wife, Sylvia Constantine, and their two daughters, Caroline and Stephanie, in 1982.[15]

Why did Barris wait until the year 1995, thirty-three years after Marilyn's death, before deciding to have the book published, which he and she had written together?

> I was in a state of shock after Marilyn died. Of course I wanted to keep our last conversations and many of her photos private. But now that I have grown older and wiser, I realize that Marilyn belongs to the public and her millions of fans.[16]

## Something's Got to Give

The film, which would have been Marilyn's thirtieth, was subsequently remade with a different cast and retitled *Move Over Darling*. It was released in December 1963.

## Marilyn's Legacy as a Film Star and as a Person

Stephen Marino, US Professor of English and founding editor of the *Arthur Miller Journal*, said of Marilyn:

... she, throughout her career was relegated to comedic roles which, by the way she was brilliant at. But at the time, I don't think we really considered comedic actresses as serious as actresses who would play dramatic roles.[17]

Derek Malcolm, film critic of the *London Evening Standard*, stated: '[Marilyn] wanted to be a serious actress but I think she was one of the greatest comediennes we've ever had. It's difficult to find a sexy comedienne but that was what she was'.[18]

Countless individuals and several charitable organisations had cause to be grateful to Marilyn for her kindness and generosity.

After Marilyn's death, Dr Hyman Engelberg stated:

I had several phone calls from ordinary women. The general feeling was that if they had only known Marilyn was in trouble, they would have done everything they could to help her, and so I realized that Marilyn didn't just have appeal for men. Women were aware of the lost little girl inside of her and they reacted to that.[19]

## Conclusion

Marilyn was a gifted, intelligent, and caring person, with deep sensitivity, and a poetic soul. Her lifelong need for an 'attachment figure'—a person who would love her and upon she could rely absolutely—was indicative of Emotional Deprivation Disorder, stemming from her highly disrupted and insecure childhood. All her life she longed for what she had largely been deprived of as a child: true and lasting love. It was that yearning, combined with her vulnerability, which touched the hearts of millions throughout the world.

Marilyn was also a driven person: her insecurity propelling her inexorably onwards, as, terrified of failure, she strove to perfect her craft as an actress. Of course, creativity is so often forged in the crucible of pain.

Superimposed on this was Marilyn's BPD, which held her in its grip for all of her all-too-short adult life. As she ascended each rung of the ladder of success, it inexorably dragged her back down into a world of morbid thought and suicidal ideation.

In films and photographs, she almost invariably looks radiantly happy, but this was when she was in company and therefore being distracted. When she was alone with her thoughts—thoughts that were distorted and sullied by her BPD— it was a different story. As Arthur Miller said, she required constant supervision to protect her from self-harm.

There have been endless debates over whether or not Marilyn's death was suicide. What can be said with certainty is that she died by her own hand, from an overdose of barbiturates. However, is this the whole story?

In the days before her death, Marilyn made and received several telephone calls, whereby she was in contact with Berniece and with beloved friends such as Joe DiMaggio Jr and George Barris. She also lined up future appointments in connection with her career, and she spoke on the telephone to her doctor Hyman Engelberg, who noticed nothing amiss.

Nonetheless, said Engleberg, something must have happened 'to suddenly depress her'. That something was BPD, which had stalked her for so long and led her to make several previous attempts on her own life. The disorder would now prove to be ultimately victorious.

A Marilyn Monroe who, for example, was in the company of those she loved, such as Berniece Miracle or George Barris, or who was enjoying the adulation of the troops in Korea, would not have contemplated taking her life. However, for a Marilyn alone in her bedroom, and therefore vulnerable to her BPD, it was an entirely different matter.

Was it a coincidence that both Marilyn and Gladys suffered from severe mental disorders? Although there appears to be no connection between schizophrenia (Gladys) and BPD (Marilyn), scientific studies indicate that both conditions have a genetic component.

Although psychiatrists find it convenient to compartmentalise disorders in terms of their symptomatology, real life is never quite so simple, in that there is often considerable overlap in regard to the symptoms of one disorder in relation to another. Intuitively, therefore, it is reasonable to suggest that just as there is overlap in respect of the symptoms, so there may well be overlap in respect of the genes that code for these symptoms.

Supposing that, within the genes which code for schizophrenia are to be found a portion of genes which code for BPD. If the offspring of a schizophrenic parent inherits the full complement of that parent's schizophrenic genes, then that offspring will develop schizophrenia. However, if the offspring of the schizophrenic parent inherits only that portion of his parent's geneswhich code for BPD—that offspring will develop BPD (and not schizophrenia).

Genetic research into mental disorders is still in its infancy, and the above hypothesis is purely speculative. However, if it does prove to be correct, it offers an explanation of how Marilyn may have inherited her BPD from her schizophrenic mother. Alternatively, Marilyn's BPD may have been the result of a genetic mutation that occurred within her own genetic pool.

There are many reasons why Marilyn will always be remembered. For her glamour, charm, dignity, childlike innocence, and sense of fun. However, perhaps above all, and paradoxically in the light of her own tormented existence, it is for her radiant smile and aura of happiness, which brought joy to the hearts of men and women alike. Andrew Bevan stated: 'When somebody passes away too soon, they're stuck in that time. She will always be Marilyn Monroe, 1962, to us, in our minds, and all that glamour'.[20]

# Endnotes

## Preface

1. Goodman, E., *The Fifty Year Decline and Fall of Hollywood*, (New York, MacFadden-Bartell, 1962), p.234.
2. *Ibid.*, pp. 232–3.
3. Banner, L., *MM – Personal: From the Private Archive of Marilyn Monroe*, (New York, Abrams, 2011), p. 135.
4. Monroe, M., *My Story*, (Maryland, Taylor Trade Publishing, 2007), p. 1855. Spoto, D., *Marilyn Monroe: The Biography*, (London, Chatto & Windus, 1993), p. 295.
6. Miracle, B. B., and Miracle, M. R., *My Sister Marilyn: A Memoir of Marilyn Monroe*, (Bloomington, Indiana, iUniverse, 2013), p. 189
7. Banner, L., *op. cit.*, p. 9

## Chapter 1

1. California State Board of Health, Standard Certificate of Birth.
2. California State Board of Health, Standard Certificate of Marriage.
3. Miracle, B. B., and Miracle, M. R., *My Sister Marilyn: A Memoir of Marilyn Monroe*, (Bloomington, Indiana, iUniverse, 2013), p. 60. Statement of Berniece Miracle, *née* Baker, winter 1946.
4. *Ibid.*, p. 61.
5. *Ibid.*, p. 64
6. Kennedy, J. E., and Miller, J. J., *Marilyn Monroe Unveiled: A Family History*, (New Jersey, J. J. Avenue Productions, 2016), p. 268
7. Miracle, B. B., and Miracle, M. R., *op. cit.*, p. 10.
8. *Ibid.*, pp. 64–5.
9. *Ibid.*, pp. 10–11.
10. California State Board of Health, Standard Certificate of Marriage.
11. Spoto, D., *Marilyn Monroe: The Biography*, (London, Chatto & Windus, 1993), p. 13.
12. Miracle, B. B., and Miracle, M. R., *op. cit.*, pp. 82–3.
13. Spoto, D., *op. cit.*, p. 14.
14. Barris, G., *Marilyn: Her Life in her Own Words*, (London, Headline, 1995), p. 4.
15. Morgan, M., *Marilyn Monroe: Private and Undisclosed*, (London, Robinson, 2012), p. 9.
16. Zolotow, M., *Marilyn Monroe*, (London, W. H. Allen, 1960), p. 12.
17. Miracle, B. B., and Miracle, M. R., *op. cit.*, p. 106

## Chapter 2

1. Morgan, M., *Marilyn Monroe: Private and Undisclosed*, (London, Robinson, 2012), pp. 6–7.
2. Miracle, B. B., and Miracle, M. R., *My Sister Marilyn: A Memoir of Marilyn Monroe*, (Bloomington, Indiana, iUniverse, 2013), p. 29.
3. Dougherty, J. E., *The Secret Happiness of Marilyn Monroe*, (Chicago, Playboy Press, 1976), p. 11.
4. Miracle, B. B., and Miracle, M. R., *op. cit.*, p. 5.
5. *Ibid.*, p. 5. Berniece had finally been reunited with her mother Gladys in the summer of 1946.
6. *Ibid.*, p. 38.
7. Morgan, M., *op. cit.*, p. 7.
8. Superior Court of the State of California in and for the County of Los Angeles D53720.
9. Morgan, M., *op. cit.*, p. 12.
10. Miracle, B. B., and Miracle, M. R., *op. cit.*, p. 5.
11. *Ibid.*, p. 5.
12. *Ibid.*, p. 6.
13. *Ibid.*, p. 5.
14. Morgan, M., *op. cit.*, p. 15.
15. Carpozi Jr, G., *Marilyn Monroe: Her Own Story*, (New York, Belmont Books, 1961), pp. 20–21.
16. Miracle, B. B., and Miracle, M. R., *op. cit.*, p. 5.
17. *Ibid.*, pp. 23–4.
18. *Ibid.*, p. 33.
19. *Ibid.*, p. 23.
20. *Ibid.*, p. 7.
21. *Ibid.*, p. 5.
22. *Ibid.*, p. 23.
23. *Ibid.*, p. 24.
24. www.cursumperficio.net/1962Ahtml.
25. Morgan, M., *op. cit.*, p. 19.
26. *Ibid.*, pp. 22–3.
27. Miracle, B. B., and Miracle, M. R., *op. cit.*, p. 6
28. *Ibid.*, p. 6.
29. Morgan, M., *op. cit.*, pp. 24–5. 'Hollygrove' Los Angeles County Children's Home, founded in 1880 as the Los Angeles Orphans Home Society, Los Angeles.
30. Miracle, B. B., and Miracle, M. R., *op. cit.*, p. 24.
31. Morgan, M., *op. cit.*, p. 29.
32. Kennedy, J. E., and Miller, J. J., *Marilyn Monroe Unveiled: A Family History*, (New Jersey, J. J. Avenue Productions, 2016), p. 30.
33. Morgan, M., *op. cit.*, p. 32.
34. *Ibid.*, p. 37.
35. *Ibid.*, p. 37.
36. Miracle, B. B., and Miracle, M. R., *op. cit.*, p. 17.
37. *Ibid.*, p. 8.
38. *Ibid.*, p. 13.
39. Morgan, M., *op. cit.*, p. 45.
40. *Ibid.*, p. 46.
41. Dougherty, J. E., *op. cit.*, p. 26.
42. Miracle, B. B., and Miracle, M. R., *op. cit.*, p. 24.
43. *Ibid.*, p. 17.
44. Dougherty, J. E., *op. cit.*, p. 25.
45. *Ibid.*, p. 27.
46. Spoto, D., *Marilyn Monroe: The Biography*, (London, Chatto & Windus, 1993), p. 176.
47. Banner, L., *MM – Personal: From the Private Archive of Marilyn Monroe,* (New York, Abrams, 2011), p. 166.
48. Guiles, F. L., *Norma Jeane: The Life and Death of Marilyn Monroe*, (London, Grafton Books, 1986), p. 256.
49. Spoto, D., *op. cit.*, p. 176.

50. Banner, L., *op. cit.*, p. 26.
51. *Ibid.*, p. 162.
52. Spoto, D., *op. cit.*, p. 176. Photograph from the collection of Eleanor ('Bebe') Goddard.
53. Banner, L., *op. cit.*, p. 167.
54. Guiles, F. L., *op. cit.*, p. 256.
55. Miracle, B. B., and Miracle, M. R., *op. cit.*, p. 109.
56. Spoto, D., *op. cit.*, p. 176. Photograph from the collection of Gladys Phillips Wilson.

## Chapter 3

1. Barris, G., *Marilyn: Her Life in her Own Words*, (London, Headline, 1995),  p. ix
2. *Ibid.*, p. ix.
3. *Ibid.*, p. 4.
4. *Daily News*, 23 May 1954, Marilyn Monroe: I had to Fight the Wolves of Hollywood'.
5. Barris, G., *op. cit.*, p. 3.
6. *Ibid.*, p. 128.
7. *Ibid.*, p. x.
8. *Ibid.*, p. 4.
9. *Ibid.*, pp. 4–5.
10. *Ibid.*, p. 11.
11. Goodman, E., *The Fifty Year Decline and Fall of Hollywood*, (New York, MacFadden-Bartell, 1962), p. 225.
12. Barris, G., *op. cit.*, p. 12.
13. *Ibid.*, p. 13.
14. *Ibid.*, p. 13.
15. *Ibid.*, pp. 31–2
16. 'We Remember Marilyn', MAJ Music, Inc. (ASCAP), Passport International Productions, North Hollywood, California, 1996.
17. Barris, G., *op. cit.*, pp. 31–2.
18. *Ibid.*, p. 33.
19. *Ibid.*, p. 32.
20. *Ibid.*, p. 15.
21. *Ibid.*, p. 13.
22. *Ibid.*, p. 15.
23. *Ibid.*, p. 15.
24. *Ibid.*, p. 16.
25. *Ibid.*, p. 16.
26. *Ibid.*, pp. 25–6.
27. *Ibid.*, p. 26.
28. *Ibid.*, p. 25.
29. *Ibid.*, pp. 34–5.

## Chapter 4

1. Miracle, B. B., and Miracle, M. R., *My Sister Marilyn: A Memoir of Marilyn Monroe*, (Bloomington, Indiana, iUniverse, 2013), p. 30.
2. Buchthal, S., and Comment, B. (editors), *Marilyn Monroe: Fragments: Poems, Intimate Notes, Letters*, (New York, HarperCollins*Publishers*, 2010), p. 223.
3. Carpozi, George Jr, *Marilyn Monroe: Her Own Story*, (New York, Belmont Books, 1961), p. 16.
4. Bowlby, J., *The Making & Breaking of Affectional Bonds*, (London and New York, Routledge, 1995), p. 1.
5. *Ibid.*, p. 13.
6. Bowlby, J., *Child Care and the Growth of Love*, (London, Penguin Books, 1965), p. 13.
7. *Ibid.*, p. 15.
8. *Ibid.*, p. 137.
9. *Ibid.*, p. 14.

10.  *Ibid.*, p. 46.
11.  *Ibid.*, pp. 137–8.
12.  *Ibid.*, p. 34.
13.  *Ibid.*, p. 221.
14.  *Ibid.*, pp. 13, 106–7.
15.  *Ibid.*, p. 22.
16.  *Ibid.*, p. 103.
17.  Stevenson, A., and Waite, M., *Concise Oxford English Dictionary*, (New York, Oxford University Press, 2011).

## Chapter 5

1.  Barris, G., *Marilyn: Her Life in her Own Words*, (London, Headline, 1995), pp. 23–4.
2.  *Ibid.*, p. 24.

## Chapter 6

1.  Dougherty, J. E., *The Secret Happiness of Marilyn Monroe*, (Chicago, Playboy Press, 1976), p. 16.
2.  *Ibid.*, pp. 17–18.
3.  *Ibid.*, p. 21.
4.  *Ibid.*, p. 23.
5.  *Ibid.*, p. 22.
6.  *Ibid.*, p. 27.
7.  Barris, G., *Marilyn: Her Life in her Own Words*, (London, Headline, 1995), p. 36.
8.  Kennedy, J. E., and Miller, J. J., *Marilyn Monroe Unveiled: A Family History*, (New Jersey, J. J. Avenue Productions, 2016), p. 9.
9.  Dougherty, J. E., *op. cit.*, p. 28.
10.  Buchthal, S., and Comment, B. (editors), *Marilyn Monroe: Fragments: Poems, Intimate Notes, Letters*, (New York, HarperCollinsPublishers, 2010), p. 1.
11.  Barris, G., *op. cit.*, p. 36.
12.  *Ibid.*, p. 42.
13.  Buchthal, S., and Comment, B. (editors), *op. cit.*, p. 7.
14.  Dougherty, J. E., *op. cit.*, p. 14
15.  *Ibid.*, p. 6.
16.  *Ibid.*, p. 39.
17.  *Ibid.*, p. 40.
18.  This letter, Marilyn Monroe to Grace Gifford, Van Nuys, California, dated 14 September 1942, was sold by Bonhams, L.A. on 20 April 2011.
19.  Dougherty, J. E., *op. cit.*, p. 34.
20.  *Ibid.*, p. 34.
21.  *Ibid.*, pp. 53–4.
22.  *Ibid.*, pp. 60–1
23.  *Ibid.*, p. 59.
24.  Barris, G., *op. cit.*, p. 43.
25.  Dougherty, J. E., *op. cit.*, pp. 67–68.
26.  *Ibid.*, p. 68.
27.  *Ibid.*, p. 68.
28.  *Ibid.*, p. 42.
29.  Miracle, B. B., and Miracle, M. R., *My Sister Marilyn: A Memoir of Marilyn Monroe*, (Bloomington, Indiana, iUniverse, 2013), p. 22.
30.  Barris, G., *op. cit.*, p. 44.
31.  Miracle, B. B., and Miracle, M. R., *op. cit.*, p. 40
32.  Dougherty, J. E., *op. cit.*, pp. 73–4.
33.  Barris, G., *op. cit.*, p. 44.
34.  *Ibid.*, p. 45.
35.  Dougherty, J. E., *op. cit.*, p. 84.

36. Miracle, B. B., and Miracle, M. R., *op. cit.*, p. 29.
37. *Ibid.*, pp. 30–1.
38. *Ibid.*, p. 144.
39. *Ibid.*, p. 43.
40. Dougherty, J. E., *op. cit.*, p. 79.
41. Barris, G., *op. cit.*, p. 50.
42. *Ibid.*, p. 49.
43. *Ibid.*, p. 43.
44. *Ibid.*, p. 49
45. *Ibid.*, p. 51.
46. Stevenson, A., and Waite, M., *Concise Oxford English Dictionary*, (New York, Oxford University Press, 2011).
47. Miracle, B. B., and Miracle, M. R., *op. cit.*, p. 15.
48. *Ibid.*, p. 144.
49. *Ibid.*, p. 44.
50. Goodman, E., *The Fifty Year Decline and Fall of Hollywood*, (New York, MacFadden-Bartell, 1962), p. 224.
51. Rollyson, C., *Marilyn Monroe Day by Day*, (London, Rowman & Littlefield, 2016), p. 52.
52. Barris, G., *op. cit.*, p. 81.
53. Rollyson, C., *Marilyn Monroe Day by Day*, p. 52.
54. Miracle, B. B., and Miracle, M. R., *op. cit.*, p. 48.
55. Dougherty, J. E., *op. cit.*, p. 83.
56. Miracle, B. B., and Miracle, M. R., Miracle, *op. cit.*, p. 45.
57. *Ibid.*, p. 46.
58. Dougherty, J. E., *op. cit.*, pp. 100–101.
59. *Ibid.*, pp. 87–8.
60. *Ibid.*, p. 87.
61. *Ibid.*, p. 105.
62. Barris, G., *op. cit.*, pp. 50–51.
63. Dougherty, J. E., *op. cit.*, pp. 96–7.
64. *Ibid.*, p. 103.
65. *Ibid.*, p. 105.
66. *Ibid.*, p. 98.
67. Barris, G., *op. cit.*, p. 54.
68. *Ibid.*, p. 61.
69. Miracle, B. B., and Miracle, M. R., *op. cit.*, p. 46.
70. *Ibid.*, p. 51.
71. *Ibid.*, p. 48.
72. *Ibid.*, p. 47.
73. *Ibid.*, p. 48.
74. *Ibid.*, p. 48.
75. *Ibid.*, p. 50.
76. Barris, G., *op. cit.*, p. 73.
77. *Ibid.*, pp. 63–4.
78. *Ibid.*, p. 70.
79. *Ibid.*, p. 64.
80. Miracle, B. B., and Miracle, M. R., *op. cit.*, p. 70.
81. Dougherty, J. E., *op. cit.*, pp. 108–109.
82. *Ibid.*, p. 109.
83. Miracle, B. B., and Miracle, M. R., *op. cit.*, pp. 62–3.
84. *Ibid.*, p. 62.
85. Dougherty, J. E., *op. cit.*, p. 116.
86. *Ibid.*, pp. 6–7.
87. *Ibid.*, p. 109.
88. *Ibid.*, p. 123.
89. *Ibid.*, p. 75.

90. *Ibid.*, p. 101.
91. *Ibid.*, pp. 123–4.
92. *Ibid.*, p. 128.
93. *Ibid.*, p. 122.
94. *Ibid.*, p. 133.

## Chapter 7

1. Dougherty, J. E., *The Secret Happiness of Marilyn Monroe*, (Chicago, Playboy Press, 1976), p. 14.
2. *Ibid.*, p. 28.
3. *Ibid.*, p. 30.
4. *Ibid.*, p. 31.
5. *Ibid.*, pp. 51–2.
6. *Ibid.*, p. 53.
7. *Ibid.*, p. 53.
8. *Ibid.*, p. 80.
9. *Ibid.*, p. 76.
10. *Ibid.*, p. 74.
11. *Ibid.*, pp. 33–4.
12. *Ibid.*, p. 41.
13. *Ibid.*, p. 56.
14. *Ibid.*, p. 52.
15. *Ibid.*, p. 36.
16. *Ibid.*, p. 36.
17. *Ibid.*, p. 37.
18. *Ibid.*, p. 46.
19. *Ibid.*, p. 41.
20. *Ibid.*, p. 42.
21. *Ibid.*, p. 63.
22. *Ibid.*, pp. 48–9.
23. *Ibid.*, p. 57.
24. *Ibid.*, p. 9.
25. *Ibid.*, p. 128.
26. *Ibid.*, p. 86.
27. *Ibid.*, p. 96.
28. *Ibid.*, p. 63.

## Chapter 8

1. Miracle, B. B., and Miracle, M. R., *My Sister Marilyn: A Memoir of Marilyn Monroe*, (Bloomington, Indiana, iUniverse, 2013), pp. 63–4.
2. Barris, G., *Marilyn: Her Life in her Own Words*, (London, Headline, 1995), p. 69.
3. *Ibid.*, p. 70.
4. 'We Remember Marilyn', MAJ Music, Inc. (ASCAP), Passport International Productions, North Hollywood, California, 1996.
5. Barris, G., *op. cit.*, p. 70.
6. *Ibid.*, p. 70.
7. Miracle, B. B., and Miracle, M. R., *op. cit.*, p. 70.
8. Barris, G., *op. cit.*, p. 71.
9. Miracle, B. B., and Miracle, M. R., *op. cit.*, p. 70.
10. *Ibid.*, p. 70.
11. Barris, G., *op. cit.*, pp. 73–4.
12. Miracle, B. B., and Miracle, M. R., *op. cit.*, p. 73.
13. Barris, G., *op. cit.*, pp. 70–1.
14. 'We Remember Marilyn', MAJ Music, Inc. (ASCAP), Passport International Productions, North Hollywood, California, 1996.

15. Barris, G., *op. cit.*, p. 74.
16. Spoto, D., *Marilyn Monroe: The Biography*, (London, Chatto & Windus, 1993), p. 165.
17. Miracle, B. B., and Miracle, M. R., Miracle, *op. cit.*, p. 76.
18. Barris, G., *op. cit.*, p. 79.
19. Spoto, D., *op. cit.*, p. 278.
20. Miracle, B. B., and Miracle, M. R., *op. cit.*, p. 75
21. Goodman, E., *The Fifty Year Decline and Fall of Hollywood*, (New York, MacFadden-Bartell, 1962), p. 224.
22. Goodman, E., *op. cit.*, p. 225.
23. Barris, G., *op. cit.*, p. 102.
24. *Ibid.*, p. 101.
25. Miracle, B. B., and Miracle, M. R., *op. cit.*, p. 77.
26. Buchthal, S., and Comment, B. (editors), *Marilyn Monroe: Fragments: Poems, Intimate Notes, Letters*, (New York, HarperCollins*Publishers*, 2010), p. 41.
27. Miracle, B. B., and Miracle, M. R., *op. cit.*, p. 77.
28. 'We Remember Marilyn', MAJ Music, Inc. (ASCAP), Passport International Productions, North Hollywood, California, 1996.
29. Dougherty, J. E., *The Secret Happiness of Marilyn Monroe*, (Chicago, Playboy Press, 1976), p. 123.
30. Carpozi, George Jr, *Marilyn Monroe: Her Own Story*, (New York, Belmont Books, 1961), p. 90.
31. Miracle, B. B., and Miracle, M. R., *op. cit.*, p. 78.
32. *Ibid.*, p. 82.
33. *Ibid.*, p. 82.
34. *Ibid.*, p. 82.
35. *Ibid.*, p. 83.
36. 'We Remember Marilyn', MAJ Music, Inc. (ASCAP), Passport International Productions, North Hollywood, California, 1996.
37. Miracle, B. B., and Miracle, M. R., *op. cit.*, p. 83.
38. *Ibid.*, p. 143.
39. Goodman, E., *op. cit.*, p. 226.
40. Miracle, B. B., and Miracle, M. R., *op. cit.*, p. 85.
41. *Ibid.*, p. 85.
42. *Ibid.*, p. 86.
43. Barris, G., *op. cit.*, p. 105.
44. *Ibid.*, p. 74.
45. *Ibid.*, p. 85.
46. *Ibid.*, p. 86.
47. Miracle, B. B., and Miracle, M. R., *op. cit.*, p. 75.
48. Barris, G., *op. cit.*, p. 89.
49. *Ibid.*, p. 90.
50. 'We Remember Marilyn', MAJ Music, Inc. (ASCAP), Passport International Productions, North Hollywood, California, 1996.
51. Barris, G., *op. cit.*, p. 90.
52. *Ibid.*, p. 93.
53. *Ibid.*, p. 125.
54. Carpozi, G. Jr, *op. cit.*, pp. 106–107. Marilyn Monroe to Dorothy Kilgallen.
55. Barris, G., *op. cit.*, p. 98.
56. Carpozi, G. Jr, *op. cit.*, pp. 106–7.
57. Barris, G., *op. cit.*, p. 93.
58. *Ibid.*, p. 96
59. 'We Remember Marilyn', MAJ Music, Inc. (ASCAP), Passport International Productions, North Hollywood, California, 1996.
60. Carpozi, G. Jr, *op. cit.*, pp. 106–7.
61. *Ibid.*, pp. 106–7.
62. Buchthal, S., and Comment, B. (editors), *op. cit.*, p. 187.
63. Carpozi, G. Jr, *op. cit.*, pp. 106–7.

64. 'We Remember Marilyn', MAJ Music, Inc. (ASCAP), Passport International Productions, North Hollywood, California, 1996.
65. Carpozi, G. Jr, *op. cit.*, pp. 106–7.
66. *Discovering Marilyn Monroe*, 3DD Productions, 2014.
67. Barris, G., *op. cit.*, pp. 161–163.
68. Miracle, B. B., and Miracle, M. R., *op. cit.*, p. 88.

## Chapter 9

1. Miracle, B. B., and Miracle, M. R., *My Sister Marilyn: A Memoir of Marilyn Monroe*, (Bloomington, Indiana, iUniverse, 2013), p. 82.
2. *Ibid.*, p. 87.
3. Barris, G., *Marilyn: Her Life in her Own Words*, (London, Headline, 1995), p. 102.
4. 'We Remember Marilyn', MAJ Music, Inc. (ASCAP), Passport International Productions, North Hollywood, California, 1996.
5. Barris, G., *op. cit.*, p. 106.
6. *Ibid.*, p. 102.
7. Miller, A., *Timebends: A Life*, (London, Bloomsbury, 1995), p. 358.
8. 'We Remember Marilyn', MAJ Music, Inc. (ASCAP), Passport International Productions, North Hollywood, California, 1996.
9. Barris, G., *op. cit.*, p. 112.
10. *Ibid.*, p. 106.
11. *Discovering Marilyn Monroe*, 3DD Productions, 2014.
12. Barris, G., *op. cit.*, p. 114.
13. *Ibid.*, p. 114.
14. Goodman, E., *The Fifty Year Decline and Fall of Hollywood*, (New York, MacFadden-Bartell, 1962), p. 226.
15. Miracle, B. B., and Miracle, M. R., *op. cit.*, p. 87.
16. *Discovering Marilyn Monroe*, 3DD Productions, 2014.
17. Miracle, B. B., and Miracle, M. R., *op. cit.*, pp. 91–2.
18. *Ibid.*, p. 75.
19. Buchthal, S., and Comment, B. (editors), *Marilyn Monroe: Fragments: Poems, Intimate Notes, Letters*, (New York, HarperCollinsPublishers, 2010), p. 171.
20. Barris, G., *op. cit.*, p. 114.
21. *Discovering Marilyn Monroe*, 3DD Productions, 2014.
22. Barris, G., *op. cit.*, p. 133.

## Chapter 10

1. Miller, A., *Timebends: A Life*, (London, Bloomsbury, 1995), p. 60.
2. *Ibid.*, p. 149.
3. *Artists in Love: Marilyn Monroe & Arthur Miller*, a programme by Sky Arts Production Hub, 2015.
4. Miller, A., *op. cit.*, pp. 327–328.
5. *Ibid.*, p. 356.
6. *Ibid.*, p. 385.
7. *Ibid.*, p. 386.
8. *Ibid.*, p. 379.
9. *Ibid.*, p. 380.
10. *Time* magazine: 'To Aristophanes & Back', 14 May 1956, pp. 74–82.
11. Rollyson, C., *Marilyn Monroe Day by Day*, (London, Rowman & Littlefield, 2016), p. 167.
12. Goodman, E., *The Fifty Year Decline and Fall of Hollywood*, (New York, MacFadden-Bartell, 1962), pp. 234–5.
13. Miller, A., *op. cit.*, p. 412.
14. 'We Remember Marilyn', MAJ Music, Inc. (ASCAP), Passport International Productions, North Hollywood, California, 1996.
15. Strasberg, S., *Marilyn and Me*, (London, Doubleday, 1955), p. 88.

16. Miracle, B. B., and Miracle, M. R., *My Sister Marilyn: A Memoir of Marilyn Monroe*, (Bloomington, Indiana, iUniverse, 2013), p. 152.
17. Morgan, M., *Marilyn Monroe: Private and Undisclosed*, (London, Robinson, 2012), p. 261.
18. Miller, A., *op. cit.*, p. 445.
19. Miracle, B. B., and Miracle, M. R., p. 93.
20. Miller, A., *op. cit.*, pp. 359.
21. *Ibid.*, p. 369.
22. *Ibid.*, p. 371.
23. Buchthal, S., and Comment, B. (editors), *Marilyn Monroe: Fragments: Poems, Intimate Notes, Letters*, (New York, HarperCollins*Publishers*, 2010), p. 219.
24. Miller, A., *op. cit.*, p. 435.
25. *Discovering Marilyn Monroe*, 3DD Productions, 2014.
26. Miracle, B. B., and Miracle, M. R., *op. cit.*, p. 97.
27. *Discovering Marilyn Monroe*, 3DD Productions, 2014.
28. *Ibid.*
29. Spoto, D., *Marilyn Monroe: The Biography*, (London, Chatto & Windus, 1993), p. 450.
30. Banner, L., *MM – Personal: From the Private Archive of Marilyn Monroe*, (New York, Abrams, 2011), p. 84.
31. Miracle, B. B., and Miracle, M. R., *op. cit.*, p. 98.
32. *Ibid.*, p. 99.
33. Miller, A., *op. cit.*, p. 466.
34. *Ibid.*, p. 466.
35. *Ibid.*, p. 474.
36. *Discovering Marilyn Monroe*, 3DD Productions, 2014.
37. *Ibid.*
38. *Ibid.*
39. *Ibid.*
40. *Ibid.*
41. 'We Remember Marilyn', MAJ Music, Inc. (ASCAP), Passport International Productions, North Hollywood, California, 1996.
42. *Discovering Marilyn Monroe*, 3DD Productions, 2014.
43. Buchthal, S., and Comment, B. (editors), *op. cit.*, p. 213.
44. Miracle, B. B., and Miracle, M. R., *op. cit.*, p. 156.
45. *Ibid.*, p. 92.
46. Barris, G., *Marilyn: Her Life in her Own Words*, (London, Headline, 1995), p. 117.
47. Miller, A., *op. cit.*, p. 418.
48. *Ibid.*, p.424.
49. Olivier, L., *Confessions of an Actor*, (London, Sceptre, 19820, p. 56.
50. *Ibid.*, p. 219
51. *Ibid.*, pp. 219–20.
52. *Ibid.*, p. 219.
53. *Ibid.*, p. 220.
54. *Ibid.*, p. 221.
55. Miracle, B. B., and Miracle, M. R., *op. cit.*, p. 152.
56. Olivier, L., *op. cit.*, p. 222.
57. *Ibid.*, p. 222.
58. *Ibid.*, pp. 226–7.
59. Miracle, B. B., and Miracle, M. R., *op. cit.*, p. 152.
60. 'We Remember Marilyn', MAJ Music, Inc. (ASCAP), Passport International Productions, North Hollywood, California, 1996.
61. Barris, G., *op. cit.*, p. 114.
62. *Ibid.*, p. 114.
63. *Discovering Marilyn Monroe*, 3DD Productions, 2014.
64. Barris, G., *op. cit.*, p. 114.
65. Goodman, E., *op. cit.*, pp. 232, 236.
66. Barris, G., *op. cit.*, pp. 125–6.

## Chapter 11

1. Barris, G., *Marilyn: Her Life in her Own Words*, (London, Headline, 1995), p. 126
2. Strasberg, S., *Marilyn and Me*, (London, Doubleday, 1955), p. 176.
3. Morgan, M., *Marilyn Monroe: Private and Undisclosed*, (London, Robinson, 2012), p. 307.
4. Miller, A., *Timebends: A Life*, (London, Bloomsbury, 1995), p. 507.
5. Miracle, B. B., and Miracle, M. R., *My Sister Marilyn: A Memoir of Marilyn Monroe*, (Bloomington, Indiana, iUniverse, 2013), pp. 132–3.
6. *Ibid.*, pp. 139–40.
7. Barris, G., *op. cit.*, p. 148.
8. Miracle, B. B., and Miracle, M. R., *op. cit.*, p. 133.
9. *Ibid.*, p. 136.
10. *Ibid.*, pp. 136–7.
11. *Ibid.*, p. 149.
12. *Ibid.*, pp. 150–1.
13. *Ibid.*, p. 143.
14. *Ibid.*, p. 159.
15. *Ibid.*, p. 158.
16. *Ibid.*, pp 153–4
17. Barris, G., *op. cit.*, pp. 5–6.
18. Miracle, B. B., and Miracle, M. R., *op. cit.*, p. 162.
19. *Ibid.*, pp. 162–3.
20. *Ibid.*, p. 163.
21. Barris, G., *op. cit.*, p. 143.
22. Miller, A., *op. cit.*, p. 471.

## Chapter 12

1. Goodman, E., *The Fifty Year Decline and Fall of Hollywood*, (New York, MacFadden-Bartell, 1962), pp. 230–1.
2. Barris, G., *Marilyn: Her Life in her Own Words*, (London, Headline, 1995), p. 13.
3. Miracle, B. B., and Miracle, M. R., *My Sister Marilyn: A Memoir of Marilyn Monroe*, (Bloomington, Indiana, iUniverse, 2013), p. 73.
4. Banner, L., *MM – Personal: From the Private Archive of Marilyn Monroe*, (New York, Abrams, 2011), p. 166.
5. Goodman, E., *op. cit.*, p. 229. Dahl, M., 'Your Fondest Childhood Memory May Not Have Really Happened', (New York, Science of Us, 4 September 2014).

## Chapter 13

1. Buchthal, S., and Comment, B. (editors), *Marilyn Monroe: Fragments: Poems, Intimate Notes, Letters*, (New York, HarperCollins*Publishers*, 2010), p. 2.
2. *Ibid.*, pp. 175–181.
3. Dougherty, J. E., *The Secret Happiness of Marilyn Monroe*, (Chicago, Playboy Press, 1976), p. 42.
4. Goodman, E., *The Fifty Year Decline and Fall of Hollywood*, (New York, MacFadden-Bartell, 1962), p. 232.
5. Barris, G., *Marilyn: Her Life in her Own Words*, (London, Headline, 1995), p. 125.
6. Buchthal, S., and Comment, B. (editors), *op. cit.*, p. 219.
7. *Ibid.*, p. 8.
8. *Ibid.*, p. 221.
9. Barris, G., *op. cit.*, p. 105.
10. Buchthal, S., and Comment, B. (editors), *op. cit.*, p. 7.
11. *Ibid.*, p. 221.
12. *Ibid.*, p. 159.
13. *Ibid.*, p. 221.
14. Goodman, E., *op. cit.*, p. 228.
15. Morgan, M., *Marilyn Monroe: Private and Undisclosed*, (London, Robinson, 2012), pp. 166–7.

16. Buchthal, S., and Comment, B. (editors), *op. cit.*, p. 203.
17. *Ibid.*, p. 2.
18. Goodman, E., *op. cit.*, p. 231.
19. Miracle, B. B., and Miracle, M. R., *My Sister Marilyn: A Memoir of Marilyn Monroe*, (Bloomington, Indiana, iUniverse, 2013), p. 69.
20. Buchthal, S., and Comment, B. (editors), *op. cit.*, p. 221.
21. *Ibid.*, p. 151.
22. *Ibid.*, p. 153.
23. *Ibid.*, pp. 196–7.
24. Goodman, E., *op. cit.*, p. 229.
25. Buchthal, S., and Comment, B. (editors), *op. cit.*, p. 221.
26. *Ibid.*, p. 159.
27. Miracle, B. B., and Miracle, M. R., p. 54.
28. Goodman, E., *op. cit.*, p. 229.
29. Miracle, B. B., and Miracle, M. R., p. 88
30. *Ibid.*, p. 90.
31. Barris, G. *op. cit.*, p. 113.
32. Buchthal, S., and Comment, B. (editors), *op. cit.*, p. 7.
33. *Ibid.*, p. 221.
34. *Ibid.*, p. 9.
35. *Ibid.*, p. 208.
36. *Ibid.*, p. 49.
37. Banner, L., *MM – Personal: From the Private Archive of Marilyn Monroe*, (New York, Abrams, 2011), p. 287.
38. Goodman, E., *op. cit.*, p. 224.
39. Buchthal, S., and Comment, B. (editors), *op. cit.*, p. 221.
40. *Ibid.*, p. 13.
41. *Ibid.*, p. 48.
42. *Ibid.*, p. 31.
43. *Ibid.*, p. 66.
44. *Ibid.*, p. 122.
45. *Ibid.*, pp. 226–7.
46. Rollyson, C., *Marilyn Monroe Day by Day*, (London, Rowman & Littlefield, 2016), pp. 182-3.
47. Buchthal, S., and Comment, B. (editors), *op. cit.*, p. 147.
48. Banner, L., *op. cit.*, p. 186.
49. Buchthal, S., and Comment, B. (editors), *op. cit.*, p. 223.
50. *Ibid.*, p. 221.
51. *Ibid.*, p. 221.
52. Banner, L., *op. cit.*, p. 230.
53. *Ibid.*, p. 233.
54. Miracle, B. B., and Miracle, M. R., *op. cit.*, p. 54.
55. *Ibid.*, p. 27.
56. Dougherty, J. E., *op. cit.*, pp. 52–3.
57. Miracle, B. B., and Miracle, M. R., *op. cit.*, p. 137.
58. *Marilyn Monroe: The Final Days*, Prometheus Entertainment, 2001.
59. Miracle, B. B., and Miracle, M. R., *op. cit.*, p. 5.
60. Dougherty, J. E., *op. cit.*, pp. 57–8.
61. *Ibid.*, p. 34.
62. Miracle, B. B., and Miracle, M. R., *op. cit.*, p. 98.
63. *Ibid.*, p. 1., *op. cit.*, p. 131.
64. Barris, G., *op. cit.*, p. 131.
65. *Ibid.*, p. 137.
66. *Ibid.*, pp. 137–8.
67. Dougherty, J. E., *op. cit.*, p. 123.
68. Miracle, B. B., and Miracle, M. R., *op. cit.*, *My Sister Marilyn: A Memoir of Marilyn Monroe*, p. 36.
69. *Ibid.*, p. 37.

70.  Strasberg, S., *Marilyn and Me*, (London, Doubleday, 1955), p. 88.
71.  Dougherty, J. E., *op. cit.*, p. 123.
72.  Buchthal, S., and Comment, B. (editors), *op. cit.*, p. 2.
73.  Goodman, E., *op. cit.*, p. 229.
74.  *Ibid.*, p. 224.
75.  Buchthal, S., and Comment, B. (editors), *op. cit.*, p. 114.
76.  *Ibid.*, p. 119.
77.  *Ibid.*, pp. 107, 109.
78.  *Ibid.*, p. 131.
79.  *Ibid.*, p. 127.
80.  Barris, G., *op. cit.*, p. 131.
81.  *Ibid.*, p. 106.
82.  *Ibid.*, p. 124.

## Chapter 14

1.  Bowlby, J., *The Making & Breaking of Affectional Bonds*, (London and New York, Routledge, 1995), p. 103.
2.  'We Remember Marilyn', MAJ Music, Inc. (ASCAP), Passport International Productions, North Hollywood, California, 1996.
3.  Goodman, E., *The Fifty Year Decline and Fall of Hollywood*, (New York, MacFadden-Bartell, 1962), p. 224.
4.  Goodman, E., *op. cit.*, pp. 224–5.
5.  *Discovering Marilyn Monroe*, 3DD Productions, 2014.
6.  *Marilyn Monroe: The Final Days*, Prometheus Entertainment, 2001.

## Chapter 15

1.  Morgan, M., *Marilyn Monroe: Private and Undisclosed*, (London, Robinson, 2012), p. 133.
2.  Buchthal, S., and Comment, B. (editors), *Marilyn Monroe: Fragments: Poems, Intimate Notes, Letters*, (New York, HarperCollinsPublishers, 2010), p. 210.
3.  Miracle, B. B., and Miracle, M. R., *My Sister Marilyn: A Memoir of Marilyn Monroe*, (Bloomington, Indiana, iUniverse, 2013), p.91.
4.  Buchthal, S., and Comment, B. (editors), *op. cit.*, p. 201.
5.  Rollyson, C., *Marilyn Monroe Day by Day*, (London, Rowman & Littlefield, 2016), pp. 175–6.
6.  Miracle, B. B., and Miracle, M. R., *op. cit.*, p. 91.
7.  Rollyson, C., *op. cit.*, p. 241.
8.  Strasberg, S., *Marilyn and Me*, (London, Doubleday, 1955), p. 176.
9.  Buchthal, S., and Comment, B. (editors), *op. cit.*, p. 195.
10.  Rollyson, C., *op. cit.*, p. 243.
11.  Buchthal, S., and Comment, B. (editors), *op. cit.*, pp. 207–210.
12.  *Ibid.*, pp. 208–213.
13.  Spoto, D., *Marilyn Monroe: The Biography*, (London, Chatto & Windus, 1993), p. 511.
14.  Miracle, B. B., and Miracle, M. R., *op. cit.*, pp. 100–101.
15.  Rollyson, C., *op. cit.*, p. 176.
16.  Miller, J. J., *Marilyn Monroe & Joe DiMaggio – Love in Japan, Korea & Beyond*, (New Jersey, J. J. Avenue Productions, 2016), p. 138.
17.  Morgan, M., *op. cit.*, p. 310.
18.  Spoto, D., *op. cit.*, p. 586.
19.  Strasberg, S., *op. cit.*, p. 210.
20.  *Marilyn Monroe: The Final Days*, Prometheus Entertainment, 2001.
21.  Buchthal, S., and Comment, B. (editors), *op. cit.*, p. 191.

## Chapter 16

1. First, M. B. and Ward, N. (editorial and coding consultants) *Diagnostic and Statistical Manual of Mental Disorders, Fifth Edition, DSM-5™*, (Washington DC, American Psychiatric Publishing, 2013), p. 99.
2. *Ibid.*, pp. 123–4.
3. *Ibid.*, p. 649.
4. Buchthal, S., and Çomment, B. (editors), *Marilyn Monroe: Fragments: Poems, Intimate Notes, Letters*, (New York, HarperCollins*Publishers*, 2010), p. 41.
5. *Ibid.*, p. 97.
6. *Marilyn Monroe: The Final Days*, Prometheus Entertainment, 2001.
7. Buchthal, S., and Comment, B. (editors), *op. cit.*, p. 193.
8. *Ibid.*, p. 23.
9. *Ibid.*, p. 35.
10. Stevenson, A., and Waite, M., *Concise Oxford English Dictionary*, (New York, Oxford University Press, 2011).
11. Dougherty, J. E., *The Secret Happiness of Marilyn Monroe*, (Chicago, Playboy Press, 1976), p. 63.
12. Buchthal, S., and Comment, B. (editors), *op. cit.*, p. 8.
13. Miracle, B. B., and Miracle, M. R., *My Sister Marilyn: A Memoir of Marilyn Monroe*, (Bloomington, Indiana, iUniverse, 2013), pp. 58–9.
14. Buchthal, S., and Comment, B. (editors), *op. cit.*, p. 63.
15. Goodman, E., *The Fifty Year Decline and Fall of Hollywood*, (New York, MacFadden-Bartell, 1962), p. 7.
16. *Ibid.*, p. 227.
17. Buchthal, S., and Comment, B. (editors), *op. cit.*, p. 97.
18. *Marilyn Monroe: The Final Days*, Prometheus Entertainment, 2001.
19. Miller, A., *Timebends: A Life*, (London, Bloomsbury, 1995), p. 483.
20. Miracle, B. B., and Miracle, M. R., *op. cit.*, p. 100.
21. *Ibid.*, p. 135.
22. Dougherty, J. E., *op. cit.*, p. 84
23. *Ibid.*, p. 89.
24. *Ibid.*, p. 97.
25. Miracle, B. B., and Miracle, M. R., *op. cit.*, p. 53
26. *Ibid.*, p. 142.
27. *Ibid.*, pp. 142–3.
28. First, M. B. and Ward, N. (editorial and coding consultants), *op. cit.*, p. 664.
29. Goodman, E., *op. cit.*, p. 233.
30. *Ibid.*, p. 22.
31. Dougherty, James E., *op. cit.*, p. 33.
32. Strasberg, S., *Marilyn and Me*, (London, Doubleday, 1955), p. 107.
33. Stevenson, A., and Waite, M., *Concise Oxford English Dictionary*, (New York, Oxford University Press, 2011).
34. First, M. B. and Ward, N. (editorial and coding consultants), *op. cit.*, p. 649.
35. Buchthal, S., and Comment, B. (editors), *op. cit.*, p. 2
36. *Ibid.*, p. 97.
37. Rollyson, C., *Marilyn Monroe Day by Day*, (London, Rowman & Littlefield, 2016), p. 76.
38. Strasberg, S., *op. cit.*, p. 195.
39. Buchthal, S., and Comment, B. (editors), *op. cit.*, p. 97.
40. First, M. B. and Ward, N. (editorial and coding consultants), *op. cit.*, pp. 663-6.
41. Carpozi, George Jr, *Marilyn Monroe: Her Own Story*, (New York, Belmont Books, 1961), p. 50.
42. Buchthal, S., and Comment, B. (editors), *op. cit.*, p. 139.
43. *Ibid.*, p. 19.
44. First, M. B. and Ward, N. (editorial and coding consultants), *op. cit.*, p. 665.
45. Stevenson, A., and Waite, M., *Concise Oxford English Dictionary*, (New York, Oxford University Press, 2011).

## Chapter 17

1.   Miller, A., *After the Fall*, (London, Penguin Books, 1964), p. 3.
2.   *Ibid.*, p. 5.
3.   *Ibid.*, p. 6.
4.   *Ibid.*, p. 14.
5.   *Ibid.*, p. 68.
6.   *Ibid.*, p. 70.
7.   *Marilyn Monroe: The Final Days*, Prometheus Entertainment, 2001.
8.   Miller, A., *op. cit.*, p. 70.
9.   *Ibid.*, pp. 71–2.
10.  *Ibid.*, p. 72.
11.  *Ibid.*, p. 73.
12.  *Ibid.*, p. 74.
13.  *Ibid.*, p. 81.
14.  *Ibid.*, p. 88.
15.  *Ibid.*, p. 90.
16.  *Ibid.*, p. 92.
17.  *Ibid.*, p. 94.
18.  *Ibid.*, p. 94.
19.  *Ibid.*, p. 95.
20.  *Ibid.*, p. 97.
21.  *Ibid.*, pp. 98–9.
22.  *Ibid.*, p. 102.
23.  *Ibid.*, p. 104.
24.  *Ibid.*, p.104.
25.  *Ibid.*, p. 106.
26.  *Ibid.*, p. 108.
27.  *Ibid.*, p. 109.
28.  *Ibid.*, p. 109.
29.  *Ibid.*, p. 110.
30.  *Ibid.*, p. 111.

## Chapter 18

1.   Banner, L., *MM – Personal: From the Private Archive of Marilyn Monroe*, (New York, Abrams, 2011), pp. 252–3.
2.   Stevenson, A., and Waite, M., *Concise Oxford English Dictionary*, (New York, Oxford University Press, 2011).
3.   *Diagnostic and Statistical Manual of Mental Disorders, Fifth Edition, DSM-5™*, p. 665.

## Chapter 19

1.   *Marilyn Monroe: The Final Days*, Prometheus Entertainment, 2001.
2.   *Ibid.*
3.   Miracle, B. B., and Miracle, M. R., *My Sister Marilyn: A Memoir of Marilyn Monroe*, (Bloomington, Indiana, iUniverse, 2013), pp. 164–5.
4.   *Ibid.*, p. 164.
5.   Barris, G., *Marilyn: Her Life in her Own Words*, (London, Headline, 1995),  p. 117.
6.   *Ibid.*, p. 123.
7.   *Marilyn Monroe: The Final Days*, Prometheus Entertainment, 2001.
8.   Barris, G., *op. cit.*, pp. 148–9.
9.   *Ibid.*, p. 138.
10.  *Ibid.*, p. 126.
11.  Miracle, B. B., and Miracle, M. R., *op. cit.*, p. 166.

12. *Ibid.*, p. 166.
13. Barris, G., *op. cit.*, p. 151.
14. *Ibid.*, pp. 124–7.
15. *Marilyn Monroe: The Final Days*, Prometheus Entertainment, 2001.
16. Miracle, B. B., and Miracle, M. R., *op. cit.*, p. 166–7.
17. Barris, G., *op. cit.*, pp. 132–3.
18. *Ibid.*, p. 137.
19. Brando, Marlon, with Robert Lindsey, *Brando: Songs My Mother Taught Me*, (London, Century, 1994), pp. 154–5.
20. *Ibid.*, p. 9.
21. *Ibid.*, p. 126.
22. *Ibid.*, p. 145.
23. *Ibid.*, p. 363.
24. Miracle, B. B., and Miracle, M. R., *op. cit.*, p. 168.
25. *Ibid.*, p. 168.
26. Barris, G., *op. cit.*, p. 148.
27. Miracle, B. B., and Miracle, M. R., *op. cit.*, p. 168.
28. *Marilyn Monroe: The Final Days*, Prometheus Entertainment, 2001.

## Chapter 20

1. *Marilyn Monroe: The Final Days*, Prometheus Entertainment, 2001.
2. *Ibid.*
3. *Ibid.*
4. *Ibid.*
5. *Ibid.*
6. Banner, L., *MM – Personal: From the Private Archive of Marilyn Monroe,* (New York, Abrams, 2011), p. 320.
7. *Ibid.*, p. 320–1.
8. *Ibid.*, p. 321.
9. Buchthal, S., and Comment, B. (editors), *Marilyn Monroe: Fragments: Poems, Intimate Notes, Letters,* (New York, HarperCollins*Publishers*, 2010), p. 231.
10. Winek's Drug & Chemical Blood-Level Data, 2001.
11. *Discovering Marilyn Monroe*, 3DD Productions, 2014.
12. Dougherty, J. E., *The Secret Happiness of Marilyn Monroe*, (Chicago, Playboy Press, 1976), p. 144.
13. Heymann, C. David, *Legends in Love*, (New York, Atria, 2014), p. 368.
14. Miracle, B. B., and Miracle, M. R., *My Sister Marilyn: A Memoir of Marilyn Monroe*, (Bloomington, Indiana, iUniverse, 2013), p. 198.
15. *Marilyn Monroe: The Final Days*, Prometheus Entertainment, 2001.
16. www.cursumperficio.net/1962Ahtml.
17. Mayo Clinic: Drug Addiction.
18. Prescription Drug Addiction, 26 September 2013.

## Chapter 21

1. Miracle, B. B., and Miracle, M. R., *My Sister Marilyn: A Memoir of Marilyn Monroe*, (Bloomington, Indiana, iUniverse, 2013), p. 192.
2. *Ibid.*, p. 197.
3. The *Courier-Journal*, (Louisville, Kentucky, 30 March 1941), p. 19.
4. Miracle, B. B., and Miracle, M. R., *op. cit.*, p. 186.
5. *Ibid.*, p. 196.
6. www.cursumperficio.net/1962Ahtml.
7. Dougherty, J. E., *The Secret Happiness of Marilyn Monroe*, (Chicago, Playboy Press, 1976), p. 141.
8. *Ibid.*, p. 141.

9.   Banner, L., *MM – Personal: From the Private Archive of Marilyn Monroe,* (New York, Abrams, 2011), p. 321.

10.   *Ibid.,* p. 322.

11.   Miracle, B. B., and Miracle, M. R., *op. cit.,* p. 178.

12.   Miller, A., *Timebends: A Life,* (London, Bloomsbury, 1995), p. 531.

13.   Barris, G., *Marilyn: Her Life in her Own Words,* (London, Headline, 1995), p. 153.

14.   *Ibid.,* p. 157.

15.   *Ibid.,* p. xv.

16.   *Ibid.,* p. xvi.

17.   *Artists in Love: Marilyn Monroe & Arthur Miller,* a programme by Sky Arts Production Hub, 2015.

18.   *Discovering Marilyn Monroe,* 3DD Productions, 2014.

19.   *Marilyn Monroe: The Final Days,* Prometheus Entertainment, 2001.

20.   *Discovering Marilyn Monroe,* 3DD Productions, 2014.

# Bibliography

## Books

Banner, L., *MM – Personal: From the Private Archive of Marilyn Monroe* (New York: Abrams, 2011)

Barris, G., *Marilyn: Her Life in her Own Words* (London:Headline, 1995)

Bowlby, J., *The Making & Breaking of Affectional Bonds* (London and New York: Routledge, 1995)

Bowlby, J., *Child Care and the Growth of Love* (London: Penguin Books, 1965)

Brando, M., with Lindsey, R., *Brando: Songs My Mother Taught Me* (London: Century, 1994)

Buchthal, S., and Bernard B. (editors), *Marilyn Monroe: Fragments: Poems, Intimate Notes, Letters* (New York: HarperCollins*Publishers*, 2010)

Carpozi Jr, G., *Marilyn Monroe: Her Own Story* (New York: Belmont Books, 1961)

Clark, C., *My Week with Marilyn* (London: Harper Press, 2011)

Cramer, R. Ben., *Joe DiMaggio: The Hero's Life* (New York: Simon & Schuster, 2000)

Dougherty, J. E. *The Secret Happiness of Marilyn Monroe* (Chicago: Playboy Press, 1976)

First, M. B. and Ward, N. (editorial and coding consultants), *Diagnostic and Statistical Manual of Mental Disorders, Fifth Edition, DSM-5™*, (Washington DC: American Psychiatric Publishing, 2013)

Goodman, E., *The Fifty Year Decline and Fall of Hollywood* (New York: MacFadden-Bartell, 1962)

Guiles, F. L., *Norma Jeane: The Life and Death of Marilyn Monroe* (London: Grafton Books, 1986)

Heymann, C. D., *Legends in Love* (New York: Atria, 2014)

Jensen, G. D., *Marilyn: A Great Woman's Struggles: Who Killed Her and Why* X (Dartford, UK: Xlibris, 2012)

Kahn, R., *Joe and Marilyn: A Memory of Love* (London: Sidgwick & Jackson, 1987)

Kennedy, J. E., and Miller, J. J., *Marilyn Monroe Unveiled: A Family History* (New Jersey: J. J. Avenue Productions, 2016)

Miller, A., *After the Fall* (London: Penguin Books, 1964); *Timebends: A Life* (London: Bloomsbury, 1995)

Miller, J. J., *Marilyn Monroe & Joe DiMaggio – Love in Japan, Korea & Beyond* (New Jersey: J. J. Avenue Productions, U.S.A., 2016)

Miracle, B. B., and Miracle, M. R., *My Sister Marilyn: A Memoir of Marilyn Monroe* (Bloomington, Indiana: iUniverse, 2013)

Monroe, M., *My Story* (Maryland: Taylor Trade Publishing, 2007)

Morgan, M., *Marilyn Monroe: Private and Undisclosed* (London: Robinson, 2012)

Olivier, L., *Confessions of an Actor* (London: Sceptre, 1982)

Riese, R., and Hitchens, N., *The Unabridged Marilyn: Her Life From A to Z*, (London: Corgi Books, 1988)

Rollyson, C., *Marilyn Monroe Day by Day* (London: Rowman & Littlefield, 2016); *Marilyn Monroe: A Life of the Actress* (Jackson: University Press of Mississipi, 2014)

Rosten, N., *Marilyn: An Untold Story* (New York: Nal/Signet, 1973)

Shaw, S., and Rosten, N., *Marilyn Among Friends* (London: Bloomsbury, 1987)

Sitwell, E., *Taken Care Of: An Autobiography* (London: Readers Union, Hutchinson, 1966)

Spoto, D., *Marilyn Monroe: The Biography* (London: Chatto & Windus, 1993)

Strasberg, S., *Bitter Sweet* (New York: G. P. Putnam's Sons, 1980); *Marilyn and Me*, (London: Doubleday, 1955)

Stevenson, A., and Waite, M., *Concise Oxford English Dictionary* (New York: Oxford University Press, 2011)

Taraborrelli, J. R., *The Secret Life of Marilyn Monroe* (London: Pan Books, 2010)

Zolotow, M., *Marilyn Monroe* (London: W. H. Allen, 1960)

## Film Documentaries

*Artists in Love: Marilyn Monroe & Arthur Miller*, a programme by Sky Arts Production Hub, 2015.

*Discovering Marilyn Monroe*, 3DD Productions, 2014.

*Marilyn Monroe: The Final Days*, Prometheus Entertainment, 2001.

*We Remember Marilyn*, MAJ Music, Inc. (ASCAP), Passport International Productions, North Hollywood, California, 1996.

## Websites

cursumperficio

# Index